# We Say *Shalom*

# We Say *Shalom*

## 40 WORDS TO CULTIVATE CURIOSITY AND CONNECTION

Nigel Darius

W Publishing Group
An Imprint of Thomas Nelson

*We Say Shalom*



Published by W Publishing, an imprint of Thomas Nelson, 501 Nelson Place, Nashville, TN 37214, USA.

Thomas Nelson titles may be purchased in bulk for educational, business, fundraising, or sales promotional use. For information, please email SpecialMarkets@ThomasNelson.com.

Published in association with Alive Literary Agency, www.aliveliterary.com.



ISBN 978-1-4003-5171-8 (audiobook)
ISBN 978-1-4003-5172-5 (ePub)
ISBN 978-1-4003-5169-5 (TP)

**Library of Congress Control Number: 2025943104**

*Printed in the United States of America*

25 26 27 28 29 LBC 5 4 3 2 1

*To those who choose to take their burdens
and make something beautiful . . .*

# Contents

## PART 2: EXTERNAL CONNECTION

# Introduction
# An Invitation

Our worlds are primarily comprised of messages and memories. From the moment we are moved from the womb into the world, we begin to engage in the acts of understanding and being understood.

Whether you were born beneath bright lights in a hospital room or in a warm pool of water within the walls of a home, you somehow announced your arrival. Maybe it was with a cry, or a smile, or a screech—but even without words, you began to make your message. And with emotion, compassion, and care, those involved in your arrival began to move messages right back to you.

From that moment forward, every message you have received in your upbringing has generated a new memory . . . and through the necessary acts of development and destruction, your world has been crafted through the complex puzzle of communication.

After all, this is the way that every individual understanding is created: through idea, intention, emotion, expression, learning, unlearning, and language.

To date, there are more than seven thousand known languages spoken all across planet Earth.[1]

Tribes, villages, institutions, religions, cultures, and communities all communicate with one another through known and unknown tongue. New words and nuanced expressions often arise within the cultural context of a language too—meaning that language as we know it (be it ancient or modern) is evergreen and always evolving.

As languages evolve, you would think that we as a people would too. But data would suggest that we aren't. We're actually going in the opposite direction.

I learned recently that 80 percent of Americans are monolingual.[2] This number is increasing too. The odd element about this staggering statistic is that only 40 percent of the rest of the world's population is monolingual.[3]

Think about that for a second.

Eighty percent of an entire country—a nation like America, with advanced technology, endless forms of freedom and financial opportunity, and access to a ridiculous reservoir of resources. Yet 80 percent of its people speak only one language: American English.

To magnify the matter, America is one of the most linguistically diverse countries on the planet. More than 350 languages are spoken within the American environment,[4] but, again, 80 percent of the population (as opposed to only 40 percent of the rest of the world) is monolingual.

It may come as a shock to you when you digest it, but I believe this reality is actually on-brand for the epoch we're experiencing.

We've got more technology than we've ever had, yet we're more disconnected than we've ever been. There are so many opportunities to work and make money, yet so many people are up to their necks in debt and struggling to make ends meet. We have instant access to endless information, yet we choose to scroll our pretty little lives away—dwindling our attention spans one swipe at a time. Our attention spans are now shorter than that mythologized nine-second goldfish attention span we all used to compete against in the early 2000s (humans come in at under an unbelievable 8.25 seconds).[5]

As if the 80 percent of Americans with only one learned language isn't enough, another study shows that 20 percent of American adults have only a fifth-grade literacy level.[6] In fact, that same study also states that 21 percent of adults in the United States are illiterate.[7]

So issue number one is the monolingual monarchy that we live in linguistically. Issue number two is our illiteracy. I'm not sure if you see it yet, but these two issues have created a cocktail of confusion and conflict that fosters disunity among our people.

We have crafted worlds of individualistic desire, encouraging us into an apathetic approach to understanding others.

We in the West are (for the most part) living insular lives—isolating ourselves within our echo chambers, receiving and sending the same messages over and over: "We don't need diversity," "convenience is more important than connection," "*different* means dangerous"—reinforcing our biases and fanning the flame of familiarity.

We have a tendency to rarely open our eyes until something begins to overwhelm or affect us.

We stay stuck on nasty news cycles; we silo ourselves and powwow only with people who share our political perspectives; we favor those who share the same faith we do—whether intentionally or unintentionally. When we do this, we build bias-filled silos that shelter us from experiencing the diversity and reality that exist *elsewhere.*

This ultimately decreases our margin for exploration of life outside our own.

Language is the baseline for many of our problems as a people, but the statistics I just shared give insight into much more that exists beneath the surface of our society.

All of these barriers beg the question: If you are not willing to connect across differences, how can you ever effectively communicate?

Additionally, if you do learn their language, but you misinterpret its meaning... how will you ever understand the heart of their people?

It's not just our spoken languages, though; it's also the way we listen to and interpret our experience of others. It's the way we engage and understand. It's the pain of our pasts that creates filters that we learn how to live through.

The consumption of short-form content has greatly influenced our inability to stay interested beyond quick engagement. Multi-hour podcasts, sermons preached by pastors, and full-length feature films are now chopped down into bite-size clips that lack context, making it easy for us to become emotionally charged and battered by clickbait without researching the full scope of what we see.

These acts of engagement have created a culture of continual cliff-hangers because we often abandon the research required to validate what we watch. Critical thinking and research have been reduced to an individual's interpretation of their experience as the only acceptable reality.

We have all communicated from a place of kindness and clarity only to be misunderstood by someone else. Remember, it's messages and memories. You could be sharing from a place of love but be heard and experienced through a lens of distrust and trauma—your words and actions ultimately misunderstood through a misguided baseline of belief.

This is my discovery and current conviction: Our inability to understand multiple languages and accurately interpret cultural communication is keeping us from being complete (in our person) and communally connected (as a people).

This is not an indictment of those who speak only one language; rather, it is an invitation into a deeper curiosity. The goal is not guilt but awareness, not shame but shared longing for a more connected self and a more compassionate world.

And that is the purpose behind the creation of *We Say Shalom*: to show and suggest that *language is where complexity is preserved*—that learning about languages and discovering words can rewire how we see the world.

In my love for language, linguistics, culture, communication, and community, I've comprised a book of beautiful, bite-size insights that give us a look into languages from more than ten people groups and cultures around the world. Each entry has a word that will act as a launchpad into ideas, poetry, and think pieces—offering you a chance daily to think critically, connect intentionally, and carefully approach a communal way of living.

The book is broken up into two intentional sections.

Section 1—Internal Reflection—invites you inward. Through powerful personal stories, cultural insight, and thought-provoking questions, you'll be asked to examine your inner world with honesty and curiosity. You'll confront biases and thoughts that have shaped how you steward your mode of operation. This section focuses on reshaping the way you see yourself—your patterns, your past, your posture toward growth.

Section 2 is External Connection—here, you'll turn your attention outward, stepping into stories, testimonies, and cross-cultural moments that deepen your empathy and widen your perspective. This section is an invitation to exploration, examining what it means to see your neighbor rightly and to treat them with respect as you reshape the way you see the sacred nature of our shared humanity.

These two movements—reflection and connection—work in tandem, like a call-and-response.

Together, they cultivate a new kind of language: one formed by awareness, grace, and humility. And it is through this shared language, born of inner clarity and outer compassion, that we ultimately *say shalom*—to ourselves, to our neighbor, and to the world.

So why the word *shalom*? *Shalom* is a Hebrew word. *Shalom* is a starting point of safety.

It is commonly translated as "peace" and is used in various cultures as both a greeting and a farewell. While "peace" is an accurate translation of the term, shalom implies more than just lack of conflict; it can also be translated as "completeness," "soundness," and "welfare."[8]

Shalom is applicable to an external peace between two entities—such as individuals or nations—and to an internal sense of peace within an individual.

In all facets of this life, I believe that we all long for shalom—it is what we need the most.

An internal peace within ourselves that permeates out onto other people.

This peace is influenced by the languages we've learned and is expressed through the way we live.

What words of worth we use on ourselves, we will also ease onto others.

Yet, if we live with a limited vocabulary—absent of exploration—our insecurities can become more extensive. Our confidence in our own individual culture won't be cultivated. And our desire to explore the offerings of others will ultimately evaporate.

On the contrary, all of those elements are offered to us in excess when we're willing to deal with the discomfort, embrace the unknown, and explore the worlds around us.

So today, let us receive new messages, which evolve into new memories . . . making more room for real wonder to exist within our worlds. I pray that these pages take you places and bring you peace, and that one at a time, we move from complexity to clarity, until ultimately, we say *shalom*.

# 01 Internal Reflection

Italian, kom-MWOH-veh-reh

# 01 Commuovere

To be deeply stirred, not just emotionally, but soulfully. *Commuovere* is the quiet quake within, when something unexpected brushes against your inner world and leaves it changed. A child's laughter, a story told in trembling truth, a stranger's kindness at just the right time. It is the beauty that catches you off guard, not with grandeur, but with gentleness—the kind of moment that widens your chest and makes you feel more human, more alive.

To be *commosso* (the past participle of *commuovere*) is to be undone, softly, and then reassembled with more light than you had before.

*If you have not sat with my story, you do not reserve the right to speak into it.*

Every family needs a guardian of stories—someone to conserve the unique nature and narrative of the family name.

With each word that we speak, each idea we act on, and in each tidbit of energy that we transfer to one another, we make memories that will move on to exist in the eras that arrive after us.

Our lives are the gift that we grant to generations.

Each time we press the pen to page, each time we capture a moment in our phone's camera roll, each time we invite someone else to engage in a meaningful moment—the memories we make move on into tomorrow, and at the end of these lives, we leave a legacy.

To put it poetically, I believe that each day you live, you are writing a letter (with your life) that will be read by those you leave behind.

Yet, the exploration and understanding of self (and its connection to story) is an art that's been lost due to a society of selfishness and the coddling (or co-opting) of our innate curiosity.

We believe somehow that we've just . . . arrived. Right here in these moments, with these lives, memories, material possessions, and other meaningful elements that make our lives magical.

The appreciation of our own individual stories begins when we strip them down to their most vulnerable form. When we walk back through the avenues that allowed us to arrive.

The inflection point for my identity occurred in 2020, right at the beginning of the pandemic.

I had just published my first book—a huge feat for any independent author or artist. The engagement was exhilarating. The story I shared sent shock waves through the cultural moment, connecting people in ways I could've never imagined, but the greatest connection made in this very interesting and intimate time was the connection that I made with my mother, who taught me about my life through my family line.

My first book was a book of poetry and art. It gave a nod to the kitchen table in my childhood home—one often abandoned and rarely eaten at. It was the table where we stacked papers and projects and stole chairs to take to our rooms when friends were over to spend time in front of the television. I inquired through my content about Humanity's Table—curious as to whether people appreciated their own stories enough to extend invitations to others to come sit and, in the discomfort of sharing, curious about who was willing to stay.

Sharing stories became a regular practice for my family and me during the pandemic. We'd call one another often and just recall moments from the past, reminiscing on reality.

A week before the book was released, my mom got her own copy, and after reading the introduction and a handful of poems, she picked up the phone and called me crying.

Through tears and subtle sobs, she shared, "I know that you don't know this, but my poetry was published once too. When I was thirteen or fourteen, one of my pieces was picked up and published in a handful of places. I'll send you some pictures here shortly."

This not only rocked me in the moment, but it also sent me down a deep rabbit hole that I fear I've never recovered from.

If she was the poet . . . who was the preacher? If they were the preacher, who was the peacemaker? Who wrote the music, who sang the songs . . . who planted the seeds in the soil of our story?

Answer after answer started to show up. She wrote the poems; that answered the question about my affinity for writing and my desire to express myself emotionally.

Adjacent to my writing, I teach often—at churches, at corporate conferences, in workshops. Where did I get the words and the ability to articulate myself?

She reminded me of my father (who I haven't always been close to). She keyed in on his ability to communicate so effectively and shared how his father was a gospel teacher.

The same year I published my book, I began partnering with a peacemaking organization. Oddly enough, my grandmother was an activist and peacemaker, too, who advocated on behalf of marginalized people groups.

My mother was the guardian of our stories; she has been the one who has conserved the unique nature and narrative of our individual identities and family name.

I wonder how many people know their nature. I wonder how many people protect their narrative, humbling themselves and appreciating the people they came from—the ones who passed down gifts of generational gratitude to their future family members in finite forms of freedom.

Today's poem packs a bit more of a punch when you consider it in context:

***If you have not sat with my story, you do***
***not reserve the right to speak into it.***

The world screams at us daily, attempting to make us pick a side and submit to the ideas of identity that they want to impress upon us.

We were creators before we were consumers.

We were compassionate before we became capitalistic.

We had hearts of humanitarians before we became filled with hatred.

We were generous givers before we became gatekeepers.

We were *content* before we were *content*.

Divine offense develops in the heart of a human who understands their inherent identity—not one developed by consumer culture and capitalism. Not one pummeled by propaganda and political partisanship. Not one shaped by spiritual superiority or righteous indignation.

I'm afraid many of us have trotted down the trail of an identity developed by pride and not enough of our hearts have humility.

Maybe this story will act as an inflection point for your identity too.

***Our lives are letters often***
***Read once they've been lived . . .***
***Let the way you love***
***Shape a story worth reading.***

Deep roots bear great fruit, and when we dig deep enough into the past, I believe we create the opportunity to either be delighted by what we find (and understand how to use what we've been given), or to spot the source of our struggles (and find tools to uproot all that may be binding us).

Examining and understanding the past is a privilege. I pray that our hearts would be humble enough to acknowledge where we get what we've got, and (additionally) that they'll be grateful enough to give in excess (what we have) to those who need it the most.

Be careful with how you steward your story—even more so with who you let speak into it.

Our stories should be seen as sacred pages in the book of humanity, not ones meant for everyone to read, review, pick up, pick apart, and put down. Sometimes restricting access to an audience is the most intentional and honoring thing you can do for something as special, powerful, and personal as your individual story.

Shalom.

Finnish, SEE-so

# 02 Sisu

Expressing the art of extreme perseverance. Wrapped in tenacity of purpose, stoic determination, and the undeniable ability to "face even death itself."[1]

*Sisu* is the soul's marrow when everything else has burned away. *Sisu* is the quiet fire that refuses to quit—an unshakable resolve not born of bravado, but of endurance, grit, and grace under pressure. It is the deep courage to continue, even when all visible hope has vanished. More than perseverance, *sisu* is sacred defiance—the kind of strength that chooses forward motion in the face of fatigue, fear, or even death itself. It is not about ease or triumph, but the quiet heroism of holding the line when no one else can.

*Still wrestling with God.*

*Still fighting facades.*

*Still rolling the dice.*

*Still beating the odds.*

The unexpected incidents along our journey make for the sweetest, most memorable stories.

They act as something like a pause or pit stop on our journey to eternity.

William Ernest Henley famously wrote the words: "I am the master of my fate, / I am the captain of my soul."[2]

These words come from his famous poem "Invictus." And these lines slowly became a societal mantra for those seeking a center, those ushering in individual empowerment, and those who wanted to fight back against the friction of life with sheer willpower and force.

Like many other cultural colloquialisms, these words were co-opted and lived out of context. The world began to inhabit these lines without understanding their origin, turning Henley's meaning into a narrative of their own. Many of us do this in our own lives with the labels we live by. We let a tragedy or trauma define us; we take our brokenness and wear it like a badge, building it like a brand. We let titles tell us who we are and who others are not. In doing so, we improperly contextualize our character, building boundaries and living within their limitations.

Henley's entire poem has to do with perseverance. Henley encourages himself to remember who he is amid the unwavering, unrelenting chaos of the seas before him. He isn't saying he's in control; it's actually the opposite—that he couldn't be more out of control—yet he holds an internal equanimity against all odds.

Let me put a spin on his perspective today . . . with a poem:

***I'm not the master of my fate,***
***I'm not the captain of my soul***
***I am the subject of my limitations***
***And there is much I can't control.***

The poem (that I politely remixed) can be a beautiful baseline for each of us to remember today. In a world where many claim to manifest their every opportunity; in a world where the intention is to insert self on the throne of our collective heart; and in a world where everyone has somehow "bootstrapped" everything, remember:

You did not arrive at who you are, how you are, or where you are . . . alone.

If we have so much control, why aren't we able to predict or prepare ourselves for the unforeseen and inconvenient?

Even with all of our intuition and innate rhythms, we still make missteps . . . and without God as a guide, would we ever learn to dance?

I have arrived at this idea—life with God is a tumultuous two-step of mystery.

You and I, as we learn to dance, have no choice but to fall and fail.

To step on our partner's toes.

To goofily get back up after ruining all that we've rehearsed.

To sometimes opt out due to exhaustion.

The two options (often at hand) are to keep dancing or get off the dance floor. And although I invite you to fall in love with the former, I know that the latter lends benefits of its own as well.

Missteps make for maturity.

Failure leads to lessons learned.

Rolling the dice and risking it all may make for a mighty reward.

Humility, however, comes from needing someone to hold your hand and help you.

The dance of life is patience, but we've been persuaded to believe that it is performance.

The questions I want you to ask yourself today are: What or who is pressuring you to perform? What or who is pressuring you to perform *perfectly*? Why is your hyper-independence taking precedence over your ability to ask for help?

After answering these questions—if you're even able to at all—I want you to stop and remind yourself that stumbling is a part of the practice. That swollen ankles come equipped with the act of dancing. That the art of your life (internal and external) is shaped by mistakes and misfortune just as much as it is by achievement and accolade.

Tomorrow has worries of its own.

We ought to speak this over ourselves when days on the dance floor feel daunting.

When the two-step with God comes with more work and whiplash than it does with joy and jazz.

When it all seems too overwhelming. When success slows up. When the effort put in isn't met right away with reward.

It's essential to take a deep breath, take time to decompress, and be intentional about deconstructing whatever issues exist at the moment . . . because bad days don't last forever and every season has to change.

It's in the fruit of our frustrations that we find the power to persevere.

Keep dancing.

Shalom.

Latin, VULL-nus

# 03 Vulnus

The Latin word *vulnus* translates to "wound" or "injury." It refers to something that has been torn, harmed, or pierced. It is the origin of the English word *vulnerable*, which stems from the Latin *vulnerabilis*—a combination of *vulnus* (wound) and the suffix *-abilis* (able to).[1] This connection inherently ties vulnerability to the capacity to be physically and metaphorically wounded.

*Vulnus* has significant connotations in ancient Roman texts, often symbolizing both physical injuries and emotional or psychological harm.[2] Its usage conveys a sense of exposure, openness, and fragility—qualities that make one susceptible to pain but also highlight a profound human reality: the ability to feel deeply and connect meaningfully.

*We would rather sow*

*stitches of secret inside us,*

*than undo the seams that*

*build borders and bias.*

One cold morning in McAllen, Texas, I'm in a rental car heading back to the airport, embarking on the long journey home to Atlanta. I'd been in Texas for work—hosting a handful of events for Chick-fil-A at several grand openings for restaurants just minutes from the border of Mexico.

I always relish the ride back to the airport because I'm leaving a sea of experiences wherever I've stayed. I take home the memories in heart and mind, no matter how bad or beautiful.

This trip had been special, too, and just when I thought the trip's memories had ended, I encountered an experience that I would never forget.

AirPods in, I'm making my way through the bustling airport and see a slew of people sitting at the airport bar—two women in particular who seem to be *at least* several drinks in.

I normally wouldn't pay attention to something of the sort, because this is a very on-brand instance for airport bars, but they were *really* making a commotion and carrying on—so loud that their hoots and hollers could be heard over my songs.

I kept stepping, although silently annoyed, and made my way past security to the boarding gate.

Thirty minutes or so pass, and as we're finally piling into the plane . . . guess who shows up?

The two women who were wilding out at the airport bar!

It was everything you thought it would be and then some.

My perspective shifted from annoyed to *aware*—understanding that beneath the surface of any intoxication, there is typically a silent story being told, and that was exactly what I was experiencing while taking my seat on the plane.

A small boy and his mother take the two seats next to me: the boy in the window seat, his mother in the middle, me (with the small bladder) at the end, in the aisle seat. Just two rows back, over my left shoulder, sit the intoxicated individuals who are not only continuing to carry on but are also beginning to pull out small airplane bottles of vodka to consume before we take off into the clouds.

Simultaneously, I'm in the middle of two stories—the mother of the small boy leans over to me and says: "I just want to let you know that my son has autism, and planes *really* excite him. At any point from takeoff to touchdown, he can get a little animated. I just thought you should be warned."

I take a deep breath and buckle my seat belt, sweetly acknowledging the story and assuring her that everything will be fine.

At the same time that she's sharing the story about her son and his excitement, the two intoxicated women two rows back begin sharing with nearby passengers that they've been drinking all morning out of anxiety . . . and that *this is their first time ever flying.*

The silent story had now been spoken out loud, but these two women had no idea that their experience was about to be everything they expected it to be . . . and then some.

The cabin has been prepared for takeoff. The flight attendants have shown us how to put on our seat belts and shared where we could find oxygen masks if anything goes awry while we fly.

We watch the preflight promotional video.

We roll down the tarmac at top speed to take off, and we're successfully in the sky.

At about ten thousand feet, we hit a really, *really* rough patch of air.

The plane starts shaking, the women start screaming, and the young boy with autism in the window seat puts the funniest exclamation point imaginable on the moment when he begins to scream: "CRASH! CRASH! CRASH!"

I have laughed till I've cried many times in my life, and this time was one that I will never forget. My stomach in pain, tears in my eyes from laughter, barely breathing from the funny—I gather myself, turn around to console the women, and softly say: "The best thing that you can do right now is look down."

*What is comedic to some, may be dramatic to others.* This was a moment of duality wrapped in the power of perspective.

I wanted to reassure these passengers (and also give them a raw dose of reality) that we are *all* deeply out of control . . . and that's okay.

I can't help but pull out for each of us the powerful parallel between those two women, their anxiety, and the experience we embark on when we board an airplane.

We pile into the plane, put away our luggage, listen to instructions, and trust men or women (whom we sometimes can't even see) to professionally fly giant pieces of heavy metal across the earth (in all its conditions) and place us from point A to point B.

Some of us are being eaten alive right now with unnecessary anxiety.

We're white-knuckling our way through life, worrying about things that we can't control.

We're giving power to possibilities that don't exist and expecting outcomes that may never happen. Building narratives in our minds that are filled with mayhem and misery, when we could begin to flip the script on our scenarios and look out the airplane windows with wonder, seeing that we're soaring through cotton-candy clouds that are calling out for our curiosity, between beautiful blue skies and serene sunsets.

The notion I'm inviting you into isn't easy to accept or embrace, and it also doesn't neglect the fact that our bodies naturally respond to scenarios we're uncomfortable with or instances we're not naturally immersed into.

In fact, I used to be just like the women I'm referring to in this story—so consumed with the ongoings and inner workings of the airplane that I refused to open my window and accept the fact that I was speeding through space, a passenger on a plane with an unknown pilot, utterly and completely out of control.

Accepting that the only things I can change are my emotions and my mind.

And this is the difficulty of adulthood: Many of us are afraid to look into the mirror or simply stare out the window for a while. And in our inability to accept our reality, we neglect that there is much undoing required to evolve.

When I think about undoing, I always return to a conversation that I had with my father when I was a teenager. He said: "Nigel, the older we get, the more work we must do so that we don't become stuck in our ways."

He was speaking to a certain kind of suffering that happens *collectively* when we're obsessed with the preservation of our own individual ideas and identity.

Vulnerability is a heavy-laden part of the luggage that we all carry in our lives, whether we acknowledge it or not. Like the women trembling at turbulence or the mother calmly explaining her son's excitement, we each confront the world from our unique vantage points—fragile, exposed, and hopeful.

But in truth, isn't this what makes life so profound?

To feel deeply, to laugh amid chaos, to extend grace when others unravel—these are the stitches that bind the human experience.

Life's turbulence reveals something sacred: Our wounds don't make us weak; they make us wonderfully human. In our surrender to the uncontrollable, we discover a resilience that doesn't come from resisting life but from embracing its raw, unpolished beauty.

The shaking plane, the crying child, the women who carried their fear to the skies—all were reminders that courage isn't the absence of fear but the willingness to face it, perhaps even laugh in its presence.

And so, I invite you to take a moment to let go.

Release the grip of imagined disasters and step into the freedom of trust—not blind faith but a quiet assurance that even in life's messiest moments, there's beauty to be found.

Open the metaphorical window and gaze out at the clouds that call to your curiosity. Allow yourself to marvel at the surreal wonder of simply being alive, carried through the vastness by forces you don't control but can still find peace within.

Let your wounds be not a sign of brokenness but of openness—a reminder that in every tear and every seam, there's an opportunity to connect, to laugh, to heal, and to grow.

Vulnerability isn't a condition to be fixed but a gift to be embraced. Look down, look out, or simply look within—your perspective can transform the journey into a thing of beauty.

Shalom.

German, EE-lent

# 04 Elend

Translated as "native displacement," the Germanic term *Elend* carries a deep, haunting resonance—one that speaks to a condition far beyond mere suffering. It originally referred to exile, foreignness, or being away from one's homeland—a state of displacement both physical and existential.

It described those who were forced into exile, wandering strangers in unfamiliar lands—disoriented and homesick. Over time, the term evolved into a broader expression of misery and destitution, reflecting not just geographic dislocation but also the deep-seated agony of being cut off from one's place, people, and sense of rootedness.

*Masked in marvel is the*

*might that you may find*

*as you stroll all alone*

*amongst the wilderness.*

What if the feeling of displacement was not an ending but a beginning? What if longing could be more than an ache—what if it could be a doorway?

I consider this when I examine the full scope of what it means to be human: a journey marked by its ability to imagine something beyond what is, to dream of home—even in the wilderness.

Christianity is a name spoken in many tongues, worn on many hearts, and often burdened by many misconceptions. It has been both a beacon and a battleground—a faith whispered in the secret corners of history and shouted from the platforms of prosperity. Some know it through the Christ of Scripture, some through the lens of cultural expectation, and others through the late-night glow of televangelists seeking something other than souls.

This faith, profound in its depth and wide in its reach, has been distilled into verses etched onto eye-black, stitched onto wristbands, and captioned beneath Instagram selfies (or placed in bios). Hobby Lobby stores across America house framed scriptures, engraved wooden plaques, and banners that declare the words of Jeremiah 29:11: "'For I know the plans I have for you,' declares the LORD, 'plans to prosper you and not to harm you, plans to give you hope and a future.'"

Yet words without context become hollow. Like Philippians 4:13—so often quoted as a promise of individual triumph rather than a statement of enduring faith—Jeremiah 29:11 has been detached from its original terrain. It is a verse that speaks not of immediate comfort but of resilience through exile, of a people displaced, commanded not to escape their suffering but to root themselves within it.

Exile is not always a deviation from the plans of God.

Sometimes, it's actually the epitome of His plans.

The Israelites were called to build, to plant, to dwell—to transform a foreign land into a place of flourishing. The promise of hope was real, but it was not immediate. It required endurance, a reshaping of identity, and a willingness to live within the tension of displacement.

And so it is with us.

We, too, walk as exiles in a world that feels fragmented. We see the fractures—polarized politics, unanswered cries of genocide, leaders who exploit rather than uplift. The weight of this reality can be suffocating, but *Elend* calls us to something radical: to imagine beyond what is, toward what should be.

There is such a gift in losing control.

When our hands are emptied of the things we once clutched tightly—plans, comfort, the illusion of certainty—we are left with the only thing that was ever real: God's presence. The less we command, the more we are invited to trust. The wilderness strips us, but it also awakens us.

We panic when the narrative we wrote for ourselves does not unfold as we envisioned.

But disappointment is not evidence of divine absence. It is an invitation—to lean in, to listen, to recognize that God is not bound by our constructs of success or ease.

Faith is not the assurance of happiness. It is the willingness to hold space for the unknown, to make peace with the discomfort of *Elend*, and to trust that displacement is not destruction but redirection.

We let our ideas, emotions, and exposure craft outcomes for stories we've yet to experience. And perhaps, in our longing for resolution, we miss the shaping work of exile—the unlearning, the reorienting, the divine reimagining of what the good life truly is.

We have been conditioned to see happiness, contentment, and comfort as markers of an abundant life. And while these things are gifts, they are not the *totality* of God.

If we want to know Him fully, we must enter every dimension of His being—even the ones that make us uneasy.

So I ask: Have you ever had a dream that did not unfold the way you imagined? A desire left unfulfilled? What if those unmet expectations are not evidence of absence but of invitation—an invitation to hold hope and tension together, to be proved right in our optimism while remaining open to God's sovereign design?

The wilderness of exile is a proving ground, but it is not a wasteland. It is the place where faith is forged, where longing teaches us to listen, and where our displacement births a holy imagination for what could be.

As you journey, remember this:

For every exile, there is a fellow sojourner.

Someone whose ache rhymes with yours.

Someone whose footsteps beat in time with your becoming.

In *Elend*, we find each other.

Not merely for comfort, but for communion.

Because even displacement can become sacred when shared.

Shalom.

(חֶסֶד), Hebrew, KHEH-sed

# 05 Ḥesed

*Ḥesed* is not a fleeting or romantic love but a faithful and steadfast love that acts. Rooted in covenantal relationships, it represents undeserved kindness and loyalty, inspiring compassionate actions. *Ḥesed* embodies a love that is enduring, reliable, and committed to the well-being of others—a love that reflects divine faithfulness.

A love that does not let go.

*Ḥesed* is covenant carved into care—not sentimental or seasonal but fierce, faithful, and rooted in action. It is the kindness that keeps showing up. The mercy that outlasts merit. Found in sacred texts and human gestures, *Ḥesed* names the divine thread woven through loyal friendship, parental devotion, and promises kept in the dark. It is love as a vow, not a feeling—enduring, generous, and utterly committed to the well-being of the other. To encounter *Ḥesed* is to witness heaven bend low and hold its shape.

*Sometimes we say*

*I love you and we don't*

*actually mean it*

*because our love*

*is best expressed*

*in what we do*

*when inconvenienced.*

In 1992, doctors confidently told my mother she would never have children.

Before receiving this news, she had already been through so much at such a young age.

After experiencing familial turbulence, being displaced, searching for solace, and praying for peace and care from her community, this news felt like a significant slap in the face. Especially for a woman pursuing abundant answers to the prayers she'd so patiently prayed.

The older I've grown, the more I've learned to appreciate how unconventional my mother's love is. It comes from a place of purity, absolutely, and I know full well that it also comes from a place of pain. What she went through to bring my brother and me into this world is unimaginable to my mind, and I would assume sometimes unbearable for her own.

As you're assuming, that 1992 news only went so far, because a few months later, in her own rebellious way, she looked impossible in its eyes and didn't ask permission to pass my brother and me into the earth.

Two miracle babies in less than two years: a divine dichotomy.

Unknowingly, this is where my relationship with time began to take shape.

Every time I pause to appreciate the beautiful miracle that my brother and I are, I examine the importance and finite nature of time.

Time has always held a different type of weight, and an immeasurable amount of meaning, to the two of us . . . because it was never supposed to be ours to experience.

By scientific standards, my brother and I weren't supposed to be here.

Think about that.

The story we share.

The spaces we've created.

The stress we brought our mother.

The Guitar Hero duels, heated *NBA 2K* and *Madden NFL* matchups.

Every last vent session and purposeful processing that has taken place over FaceTime.

And that's just the two of us . . . but it also trickles down to my individual life, and the lives of those I love and live alongside too.

Every word I've ever written or idea I've expressed. Every joke I've ever told. Every moment captured between me and my community. Every creative achievement, word of wisdom, video shared, even something as simple as small moments of laughter.

Every hug or handshake exchanged.

Every "I love you" that has left my lips or was somehow spoken to me.

It could've never been.

I don't say this in a depressive, sad way.

*I say it sentimentally* to give context to why I care so much about life, and why I love so deeply the people I've been privileged to live alongside.

In recent years, I've come to view my brother and me as *Time Thieves.*

Living on borrowed moments that, by all accounts, weren't even supposed to exist.

Every second we're here is a second we've stolen from impossibility and its odds.

For these reasons and many more, we choose to live with tenacity and rebelliously joyful spirits—taking back time and making moments as magical as we can.

Seeing our existence as part of a divine plan.

Knowing that life can't have its way, even when it tries to draw its own line in the sand.

My mother, my brother, and I are proof that miracles don't always glisten with glamour or come packed with a punch.

Sometimes, they arrive quietly.

Like a clock resetting itself.

And if you listen closely, you'll hear the tick of the seconds we keep stealing.

Because time is a gift we were never supposed to have.

So, what does this have to do with you?

What if you viewed yourself, your family, and your friends the same way?

With the finite nature of time and the fragility of humanity, why wouldn't you attempt to be present in every moment with your people, while you have them?

Why wouldn't you be patient on the first date?

Why wouldn't you look at your spouse with the same sincerity and excited eyes—the way you did in your youth—even though you've been together for so long?

Why wouldn't you stop scrolling during a film or television show to appreciate the art that someone else created for your entertainment?

Why wouldn't you live with intention and purpose, knowing the clock is ticking on all our existences, and accept that the thing that makes it meaningful is how we lean into what we love?

It's becoming more and more difficult by the day to measure how much we mean our "I love you" moments . . . because our words only mean as much as what we're willing to do when our comfort is compromised.

"I love you" holds a different type of weight when you measure its relationship to time and attention.

Oliver Burkeman said it best in his book *Four Thousand Weeks*:

> To describe attention as a "resource" is to subtly misconstrue its centrality in our lives. Most other resources on which we rely as individuals—such as food, money, and electricity—are things that facilitate life, and in some cases it's possible to live without them, at least for a while. Attention, on the other hand, just is life: your experience of being alive consists of nothing other than the sum of everything to which you pay attention.
>
> At the end of your life, looking back, whatever compelled your attention from moment to moment is simply what your life will have been. When you pay attention to something you don't especially value, it's not an exaggeration to say that you're paying with your life.[1]

The profound part of this is that all this time when we were told to pay attention, we missed the fact that the phrase quite literally means what it says.

After all, attention is the purest form of intimacy. One of the most meaningful ways that we can love someone is by giving them the thing most valuable to us—our lives.

The people right in front of us every day are worth our attention.

We ought not be people who miss the message until the messenger is missing. We ought to act in such a way that devotes days, hours, minutes, and seconds of our lives to appreciating our people while we have them.

My brother and I are miracles (to say the least), but in more than one way, many of us are miracles too. We're all living the tale of time thieves—stealing precious seconds with our people.

So, before you speak your next "I love you," stop and consider where it's coming from and why you're saying it. Handle the hard truth of how you're giving the gift of yourself to someone and why they're so special to you.

Maybe you'll see them in a way you've never seen them before, and let your actions be informed by the finite nature of time and the necessity of meaning what you say, when you say it.

Shalom.

German, fern-VEH

# 06 Fernweh

While the English word *wanderlust* captures a desire to travel, the German noun *Fernweh* expresses something deeper—a homesickness for a place you have never even seen. It is the feeling of restlessness not rooted in geography but in imagination. It speaks to the ache in us that longs for a world that does not yet exist—a place unmarred by the failures of where we've been, and untouched by the fractures of where we are.

In its essence, *Fernweh* is the ache beneath our obsessions. The thing behind the thing. The desire for escape wrapped in daydreams of perfect places, perfect people, perfect lives. Not because they are real, but because they feel better than reality.

*Just as we have*

*to close our eyes*

*before we dream, the*

*caged bird has to*

*cry before it sings.*

Many people marvel at the beauty of Manhattan without acknowledging or appreciating how much it took to be created.

When people see the skyline consisting of captivating skyscrapers, high-rise condos, and elevated experiences, they don't often think about the infrastructure beneath the beauty, or the sacrifice required to create it.

The marvel of Manhattan required death.[1]

It required taxes. It required men and women missing meals and neglecting time connecting with their families, with their friends. It required consultations and continual communication.

It took unpaid labor. It took mishaps, measuring, and cutting.

It took individuals overcoming acrophobia (fear of heights) to spend days suspended thousands of feet in the air—moving steel, connecting concrete, and wiring electrical routes from floor to floor. It took more than any man or woman could explain in one image or a million words.

And yet, we marvel at Manhattan and take our pictures of that immaculate skyline without this perspective before we post them on our socials.

I think we share a similarity with that skyline.

Our structures are continually being built upon too.

Sometimes the scaffolding looks a bit sketchy; we may spend months demolishing old parts of who we were to make room for who we are. Sometimes we're simply closed off and have no interest in inviting anyone inside to witness what awaits beyond our windows.

And sometimes we dream of other skylines entirely. Of cities we've never seen. Of lives we've never lived. Of versions of ourselves that feel lighter, freer, more understood. That's *Fernweh* at work. That sacred ache for something distant and divine.

The interesting thing about Manhattan and all its marvel, however, is that it will forever be unfinished.

Contractors don't just walk away from projects after they're finished—they'll have routine inspections, maintenance checkups, and continual oversight for quality control. No matter how built out an area or environment is, it will never arrive. In a sense, it will always be under construction—whether you see it or not.

C. S. Lewis eloquently expresses our similarities with the skyline:

> Imagine yourself as a living house. God comes in to rebuild that house. At first, perhaps, you can understand what He is doing. He is getting the drains right and stopping the leaks in the roof and so on: you knew that those jobs needed doing and so you are not surprised. But presently He starts knocking the house about in a way that hurts abominably and does not seem to make sense. What on earth is He up to? The explanation is that He is building quite a different house from the one you thought of—throwing out a new wing here, putting on an extra floor there, running up towers, making courtyards. You thought you were going to be made into a decent little cottage: but He is building a palace. He intends to come and live in it Himself.[2]

Somewhere wedged between subjectivity and serendipity, lives the strength of being seen.

And the continual fight for each of us is to know that our unseen work is inherently influenced by the idea of our external worth.

It's dangerous to derive our value from the validation of others—this is something we know. But in order for this information to become embodied wisdom, this is something we must believe.

I'm afraid many of us have become caged birds who hold the keys to our freedom, but we refuse to use them due to our unbelief.

And as I write about a city and its skyline, I'm reminded of these lines from Maya Angelou's sweet, sweet poem from decades past, which detailed the burden of the caged bird . . . the caged bird who sang.

> ***The caged bird sings***
> ***with a fearful trill***
> ***of things unknown***
> ***but longed for still . . .*** [3]

We all want someone to hear us and see us sing—to appreciate the infrastructure beneath our own individual beauty. But the eyes and ears of others appreciating us will always fall flat in the future if we never come to presently appreciate ourselves first and foremost.

And maybe that's the real invitation of *Fernweh*—not simply to long for faraway places, but to return to the sacred ground of your own becoming.

To see yourself—fully—in process.

Unfinished, yet deeply beautiful.

Imperfect, yet deeply worthy.

A skyline still under construction.

A bird still learning its song.

Wherever you go from here—whatever city you chase, whatever dream you build, whatever ache you feel—may you never forget: You are already becoming something worth marveling at.

Shalom.

(עֲרָפֶל), Hebrew, ah-RAH-fel

# 07 Araphel

*Araphel* can describe moments of deep personal struggle, when hope and transformation are hidden within despair. The sacred shadow where clarity ends and communion begins. *Araphel* is not merely darkness, but divine obscurity—a thick cloud, a holy gloom, the atmosphere in which God chooses to dwell. In Exodus 20:21 Moses enters the *araphel* to meet with God, not in sunlight, but in surrender. This is the mystery we often resist: that transformation is birthed not in certainty, but in the shrouded places. *Araphel* is the invitation to draw near through doubt, to hear God not in spite of the darkness, but because of it. The deeper the cloud, the closer the voice.

*Araphel* is the shroud of mystery where God's voice speaks most clearly, not through the absence of light but through the presence of sacred obscurity.

*Grief and hope*

*are the hug that*

*we mistake for*

*a handshake.*

Are you afraid of the dark?

That's both a question and a nod to a television show that used to air in the nineties on Nickelodeon.

A group of friends, referred to as The Midnight Society, would meet up in the middle of the woods, gather around, and tell spooky, scary stories.

As each story began, the visuals would transition into an episode that accurately portrayed their story as they told it in real time. Each time an individual shared their opening sentence of the scary story, you were transported to the world of the story to experience firsthand what they were envisioning as they wove their tale.

Looking back on my childhood, I realize how normal it was to watch TV shows like that, read scary book series like *Goosebumps*, and watch spooky movies on what seemed like almost every weekend.

I vividly remember that my brother and I would often ask our mother to put on a night-light when we went to bed . . . because we had no real proof that the creatures these writers had created weren't real, aside from the comfort that came from the words of our parents.

We would go to sleep with worries in our hearts and images in our minds of all the scary scenarios we could find ourselves within based on whatever spooky story we had heard earlier that evening.

It seemed that we were, in fact, afraid of the dark. But I wonder today if we were more afraid of the realities that *didn't* exist in that darkness. I wonder if our fears being invalidated by the light switch on the side of the wall was a humility that we weren't prepared to face.

Illumination, making our worries illegitimate—to see that, in a single second, all the worries we'd envisioned were fraudulent and far from real.

Our applied perspective informed our reality: We were taught to see darkness as something scary, to think of spirits as something satanic, to look at anything that wasn't bright or light and see it as no good and far from godly.

Until I read this quote by Barbara Brown Taylor, I had no clue that God's idea of darkness was more divine than it was depressing. Here are her lines from one of the books that saved my life, *Learning to Walk in the Dark*:

> The darkness that dominates [the story of Moses's encounter with God in Exodus 20:21] has nothing to do with what time of day it is.
>
> It has nothing to do with the position of the planets in the sky or the rods and cones in people's eyes. It is an entirely unnatural darkness—both dangerous and divine—that contains the presence of the God before whom there are no others. It is so different from what other Hebrew words mean when they say "dark" that it has its own word in the Bible: *araphel*, reserved for God's exclusive use.
>
> This thick darkness reveals the divine presence even while obscuring it, the same way the brightness of God's glory does. Both are signs of God's mercy, since ordinary human beings are not equipped to survive direct contact with the divine, in the dark or in the light.
>
> This view of darkness is far more nuanced than the one that demonizes darkness. While this darkness is dangerous, it is as sure a sign of God's presence as brightness is, which makes the fear of it different from the fear of snakes and robbers.[1]

Once more: "This thick darkness reveals the divine presence even while obscuring it, the same way the brightness of God's glory does. Both are signs of God's mercy."

If grief and hope are the hug mistaken for a handshake, then darkness is the room where the embrace takes place—gloomy, quiet, and unyielding. *Araphel*, the sacred gloom where God dwells, teaches us that darkness is not the enemy we've been conditioned to fear. Instead, it is the veil through which divine revelation comes—not despite the obscurity but because of it. Just as Moses entered *araphel* and found God, so, too, do we enter the shadowed spaces of our lives, often unaware that the very pain we resist is a sanctuary for transformation.

Just as darkness has been misunderstood in the sacred sense, it has also been demonized culturally. In America, the fear and rejection of darkness extends beyond the physical into systemic discrimination, where "darkness" became a metaphor weaponized against entire races and cultures. The fear of the dark is mirrored in the fear of the "other," rooted in ignorance and perpetuated through dehumanization.

Yet, within these shadows lies untold beauty. Just as nightfall brings a quiet grandeur and the moon casts its silver light across the earth, cultures often deemed "other" carry radiant wisdom, resilience, and creativity. The tragedy is not in the existence of the dark but in our unwillingness to step outside and witness its illumination.

Darkness, like grief, carries with it a presence that both hides and reveals, holding within it the paradox of fear and comfort, despair and divine intimacy.

For years, I mistook grief and hope as a handshake.

I viewed the two emotions as members of opposing teams who only came together at the end of regulation to shake hands and acknowledge each other on their way to the next activity.

Recent years, however, have opened my eyes to the depth of their intimacy and interconnectedness.

I'm learning that gratitude can coexist with grief.

I'm learning that the same ducts that cry tears of joy also arouse tears of anger.

I'm learning that anxiety doesn't dissipate when we reach our desired destination.

I'm learning that there is truly no cure-all for our emotional undoing.

I'm learning that all of life is healing.

It's come to my attention that grief and hope are so much more than a handshake.

Instead, they're the opposites that are attracted to one another, entangling their lives with intentionality . . . letting understanding sit at the core of their attachment.

And their understanding expresses the truth in how life is utterly imbalanced if we have one emotion without the other.

So, I have to ask: What is your idea of darkness? How do you perceive it?

Is it influenced by the ideas brought to you by cultural standards or historical connotation . . . or is it a darkness without definition, discovered through your lived experience?

I would assert to you that there is nothing to be afraid of, yet many unknowns to be understood.

And maybe that's the invitation for you today too.

Not to conquer the dark.

Not to escape it.

But to illuminate the path with curiosity and search for what is inside it.

Where, in your own life, have grief and hope been sitting closer than you realized?

What spaces—that once felt unbearable—might now hold traces of God's mercy?

What stories have you told yourself about the dark . . . that might no longer be true?

Could it be that the very thing you thought was proof of God's absence . . . is actually evidence of God's nearness?

Maybe this is less about seeing in the dark and more about trusting that you are seen within it.

That whatever area of life you are experiencing *araphel*—your shadowed place—is not a punishment to endure, but a sanctuary to enter.

Maybe the darkness isn't asking you to be brave.

Maybe it's asking you to be still.

Shalom.

(改善), Japanese, KAI-zen

# 08 Kaizen

The quiet pursuit of intentional progress. *Kaizen* is the belief that lasting transformation is not born in bursts but in small, steady steps—deliberate movements toward wholeness.

Rooted in postwar Japan and adopted by businesses, it is more than strategy: It is a philosophy.

A way of life that trusts in the power of accumulation—that every tiny change, repeated over time, becomes momentum. *Kaizen* invites us to resist perfectionism and embrace process: to show up again and again with intention. Not for the sake of constant striving, but sacred becoming.

*It doesn't have*

*to be perfect*

*to be powerful.*

Every Christmas in my childhood home carried its own meaning. Every other year, we adopted different family traditions—taking pictures, recording home videos, opening presents early, and preparing meals large enough to last for days.

Wish lists were written, though there was never a promise that what we wished for would appear beneath the tree. We were raised with the idea that family meant more than anything material, and this was earnestly lived out over the years.

But as I began to age and mature each year, Christmas began to mean different things to me.

It meant more intentional time with family after coming to the realization that everyone is aging.

My parents divorced, and that came with two different types of Christmases. It meant spending some Christmases alone for the sake of my own sanity.

Each year, it had less to do with the gifts we received and the way we gathered and more to do with the intentions and actions we could consistently show up with.

It became all about intention—a time to notice the quiet acts of love that often went unseen.

One of those acts came faithfully from my Aunt Joy. Every Christmas, without fail, she would drive two hours through snow and ice to bring her nephews simple gifts: socks, T-shirts, tins of popcorn, and snacks—essentials you don't understand or desire as a child but come to appreciate as you get older.

However, the most memorable gesture would come a month or two later, when she sent handwritten letters attached with five-dollar bills tucked inside for my brother and me on our birthdays.

Year after year, for thirty-two years, my Aunt Joy has never missed a single Christmas or birthday.

At first glance, five dollars seems almost laughable in today's economy. It's not enough to fill a tank of gas or even buy a full meal. But when I think about her intention, I see the power of her words—*I love you, I support you, I see you,* and *I am here for you.* The worth of those words was embodied in her actions—specifically in her showing up consistently, for thirty-two years straight.

Over time, her acts and their significance became immeasurable.

My brother and I have spent that money on everything from essential everyday needs to tithing money into church collection plates, helping the unhoused, and tipping our waiters.

Aunt Joy's five-dollar gifts were not just money; they were investments in us—small acts of consistency that carried a legacy of care and generosity.

This is *kaizen* in its purest form: the idea that small, intentional actions, repeated over time, create lasting impact. Like Aunt Joy's five-dollar bills, each small gesture may seem insignificant on its own, but their cumulative effect changes lives.

Philosophically, *kaizen* reminds us to embrace the process, recognizing that who we become and how we behold lie not in monumental achievements, but in faithful consistency to the small things we commit to.

Growing up in church, we talked a lot about being thankful for our daily bread. There's no shame in aspiring toward the big stuff and praying that God's power would grace us with such gifts, but we should also make a regular practice of gratitude for the beautiful, abundant blessings that we're holding on to today.

Each year when Aunt Joy's envelopes showed up in the mail, I was always caught by surprise. It was sweet and special to receive her small gifts, but they always came packed with such a powerful punch. They honestly remind me of God's faithfulness.

He works in the unseen moments of our lives, the daily acts of grace and mercy that slowly transform us into His likeness.

Whether we acknowledge it or not, God is always at work in us—refining us step-by-step. We don't need to make dramatic leaps to please Him or be settled within ourselves. In fact, I've found that our efforts often exist to ease our ego.

This is why we need to observe and implement *kaizen*.

*Kaizen* is formed from *kai* (改), meaning "change," and *zen* (善), meaning "good" or "better."[1] Together, they represent the philosophy of "change for the better" through small, intentional steps. While often applied to business and productivity, *Kaizen* extends far beyond the workplace, teaching us that true growth—whether personal, relational, or spiritual—is rooted in consistency and deliberate effort.

*Kaizen* invites us to embrace patience. Progress is not a leap but a journey made up of countless small actions that seem insignificant in the moment yet yield profound transformation over time. This philosophy echoes deeply in the rhythms of life, where even the smallest acts of kindness and discipline ripple outward, shaping a better world.

*Kaizen* mirrors God's design for our lives. Sanctification—the process of becoming more like Christ—is not a one-time event but a gradual, lifelong journey.

Philippians 1:6 assures us: "He who began a good work in you will carry it on to completion until the day of Christ Jesus." God works in the small moments, the quiet acts of faithfulness, to mold us into His masterpieces.

So today, here is our challenge: to see leaps not as singular moments but as the cumulative effect of thousands of small, deliberate steps. What small actions can you take today to invest in others? How can you cultivate soil that nurtures growth—not just in your life but in the lives of those around you? What perspectives need to be reshaped so you don't slip into shame when success doesn't look like you thought it would?

Life may live at the end of the leap. But it's not always the giant, life-altering leap that we should be looking for. Instead, we can slowly serve ourselves and others through our altar of intentions, built through the little leaps we take in our everyday lives through the countless unseen steps.

Shalom.

(רָכַךְ), Hebrew, rah-KAHK

# 09 Rakak

The Hebrew word *rakak* carries a depth that goes beyond a simple call to kindness. It speaks to a posture of the soul—a softness that refuses to be hardened by the weight of the world. In ancient Hebrew thought, *rakak* is not just about being gentle in action but about being tender in essence. It is the heart that remains pliable, able to respond to others with grace rather than resistance.

This word appears in the scriptures as an invitation to cultivate divine empathy—to remain open, to allow our spirit to be moved, to let love be the shaping force behind our words and our ways.[1] A heart that is being *rakak* is one that does not retreat into cynicism but leans into compassion, even when met with hostility.[2]

*Sometimes it feels*

*like we're all*

*playing a game*

*called Race You*

*to the Red Light.*

In a culture that rewards sharp edges and quick reflexes, where efficiency is prized over empathy, *rakak* reminds us that true strength is found in tenderness—possessing a strength so sure of itself that it does not need to wield force.

A heart that is still able to break is a heart still able to love. A spirit that remains soft in the presence of pain is one that understands the nature of God. This is the kind of humanity that remains moldable in the hands of God—resisting the temptation to become calloused.

I have learned the weight of this truth by watching the years unfold with careful attention.

Observing time has become a sacred practice—one that pulls me away from distractions and into the presence of what is real.

Brother Lawrence put it best:

> The holiest and most necessary practice in the spiritual life is that of the presence of God.[3]

God always speaks to me through sequential moments, small stamps in time that, when strung together, form a story worth telling. This is how I have come to name my years—each one marked by a word, a scripture, an unfolding revelation. Last year, that word was *time*.

I had spent so much of my life frustrated by delays, tangled in the tension between ambition and surrender. But as the days passed, I began to realize that my frustration had less to do with unmet goals and more to do with my own fleeting mortality. The rush I felt wasn't about reaching a destination—it was about my fear of running out of road.

At the start of the year, God gave me Ephesians 5:15–16: "Be very careful, then, how you live—not as unwise but as wise, making the most of every opportunity, because the days are evil."

So I asked myself: Why are the days evil?

We often think of evil as an external force, something outside of ourselves. But what if evil is also the slow erosion of tenderness? What if it is the incremental hardening of the heart—the quiet dismissal of what is sacred?

The world is imperfect, but within its imperfection lies opportunity.

A perfect world would require no faith, no growth, no dependency on God. But imperfection calls us to action—it is an invitation to engage.

And if something unsettles you, if an injustice or a fracture in the world tugs at your spirit, perhaps that is an indication that you are called to tend to it.

***If it's yours to see, it may be yours to serve.***

It is easier to comment than to contribute, easier to critique than to create. But judgment is an injustice to the call of curiosity.

In the garden, after humanity's first failure, God did not start with condemnation—He started with a question: "Where are you?" (Genesis 3:9).

He knew, and yet He still asked. He invited Adam and Eve to locate themselves, to engage in their own becoming.

We are often too quick to place judgment where God would place inquiry.

And when we close ourselves off to curiosity, we rob ourselves of the ability to understand, to grow, to be transformed.

If we are not beyond repair, then the world is not beyond redemption.

God's work is not about behavior modification—it is about *progressive sanctification.* A slow unfolding, a deep transformation, a gentle remaking.

> ***Our desires should not be* achievement-oriented *but* presence-driven*—not about ticking off spiritual milestones but about dwelling in the unforced rhythms of grace.***

We ought to operate with eternal intentions. Seeing the world through earthly eyes will always lead to limitation. But *eternal eyes envision justice, beloved community, and redemption.* They understand that while we cannot change the entire world, we can change individual worlds. This is why we are here—not for status, not for self-glory, but for service.

Because the truth is, we are running out of time.

Not in a way meant to induce fear, but in a way that should awaken urgency.

A call to return to tenderness.

A call to presence.

A call to *rakak.*

I've come to believe that the most important thing we can do with our days is not to chase success but to cultivate sensitivity—to practice the presence of God over the pursuit of preference.

The world does not need more hardened hearts.

It needs people who are willing to remain tender, willing to let love shape them, willing to ask, *Where am I?* and listen for the divine whisper in response.

Shalom.

English (from the late Latin *genuflectere*), JEN-yoo-flekt

# 10 Genuflect

The act of bending the knee as a sign of reverence, often in religious or symbolic contexts.

*Genuflection* is more than a physical act; it is a posture of the heart. Historically, it has symbolized submission to a higher power, humility in the presence of something greater, and deep respect for sacred spaces. In faith traditions, bending the knee is an outward reflection of an inward surrender—a recognition that some things in life are too vast to control, too holy to approach without honor.

To bow is not to shrink—it is to acknowledge something greater, something worth yielding to. And in doing so, we find strength, clarity, and a path forward.

*You may not be the cause,*

*but you are called*

*to be the cure.*

There is a thin line between humility and shame, and often, we mistake one for the other.

I have learned in my lifetime that the voices of our past are always trying to inform our future and the way that it is supposed to feel.

Just ask the Israelites.

A people enslaved for generations, crying out for deliverance. And when their deliverance came, it didn't arrive as they had imagined. Freedom required faith. It required walking into an unknown wilderness, step-by-step, with no clear vision of what was ahead.

Shackled, beaten, and broken down, they spent years crying out to God . . . and finally, He answered. He sent them a deliverer. He sent them a promise. And when they stepped into freedom, when they began their journey toward everything they had prayed for, they hesitated. They grumbled. They doubted. They said they'd rather go back to Pharaoh than press through the wilderness—even though the wilderness was the only way to the promised land.

It wasn't just their bodies that had been enslaved—it was their minds too. Their identity had been formed in oppression, and when God called them out of it, they didn't know how to walk in the freedom they had been given.

This isn't just an issue of antiquity. It's a story I've seen replayed generationally, in myself . . . and among the people I love.

I've watched people who are born to break generational cycles hesitate when they felt the weight of that responsibility.

People who were meant to stand tall but mistake bowing their heads in shame for humility. People who apologize for their gifts, thinking they must earn the right to take up space.

How often do we cling to what's familiar, even when it's harmful?

Simply because we know that stepping into something significant feels so uncertain.

How often do we confuse meekness with smallness, acting as if shrinking ourselves is a virtue?

The question isn't just how often—it's also, how long? How long will we wait to walk?

How much time do we waste in our own wilderness?

How often do we hesitate in pursuit of the very thing we prayed for?

James Baldwin once said:

> What is it you want me to reconcile myself to? I was born here, almost 60 years ago. I'm not going to live another 60 years. You always told me it takes time. It's taken my father's time, my mother's time, my uncle's time, my brothers' and my sisters' time . . . How much time do you want for your progress?[2]

His words were about justice, about the ever-moving goalpost of equality.

But if we have ears to hear, they apply to us too.

How much time will fear take from you?

How many years will hesitation steal?

How many generations will bow in false humility while waiting for clarity that only comes in motion?

Time and time again, God calls unqualified people and tells them to go anyway. And time and time again, those people hesitate, their self-doubt screaming louder than the voice of the One who sent them.

True humility isn't about playing small.

True humility is about surrender—about recognizing that our calling isn't about us, anyway.

*Genuflection* is about reverence, but what are we really bowing to? Are we bowing to God, or are we bowing to our insecurities? Are we kneeling in worship, or are we kneeling because we're afraid to stand? Are we embarrassed and in disbelief at God when He redeems time through using us as the ones to reconcile the gaps within our family line?

*Genuflection* is not just about how we respond to God—it's also about how we show up for each other.

Jesus shared sentiments of how we show up for one another during a contentious conversation with His disciples. As the disciples were arguing about who would be the greatest among their group, He interjected with intention and said: "The greatest among you will be your servant" (Matthew 23:11).

And today, I believe that that's also the invitation for us—to bend not in shame but in service. To act not with an agenda but with intention.

To kneel beside someone in their sorrow, to stand in the gap for a friend, to offer your presence not as a performance but as a posture of love.

We don't just glorify God in solitude—we glorify Him in how we see others.

In how we walk with them through their wilderness.

In how we call them forward when they forget who they are.

True *genuflection* toward God will always ripple outward as compassion toward others.

This is the kind of reverence the world is starved for—not just holy moments in sacred spaces, but sacred postures in everyday relationships.

The Israelites eventually made it to their promised land, but not without a process.

Not without pressing through the wilderness. Not without shedding the remnants of who they were under Pharaoh so they could step fully into who they were under God.

The same is true for us.

So maybe the question today isn't whether we feel ready. Maybe the question is whether we'll trust the One who called us—whether we'll stand, even when our knees are trembling. Even when our disbelief is dancing around our mind, making us believe that we don't deserve to be delivered to our divine destinations.

Maybe, just maybe, *genuflection* isn't about shrinking ourselves.

Maybe it's about bending the knee, catching our breath, and then standing up—taller, freer, and more ready than we ever believed we could be.

Shalom.

(תְּהוֹם), Hebrew, teh-HOME

# 11 Tehom

A Hebrew word referring to the deep, abyss, or great depths of the earth and sea.

The word *tehom* first appears in Genesis 1:2, describing the formless void before creation—"Darkness was over the surface of the deep [*tehom*], and the Spirit of God was hovering over the waters." It represents chaos, the unknown, the depths beyond human reach.

In ancient Jewish thought, *tehom* was not just a physical reality but a spiritual one—the deep spaces where mysteries reside, where storms rage, where God's presence is either felt profoundly or seemingly absent. *The abyss is both terrifying and transformative.*

*Some scars share truths*
*that our mouths could*
*never speak of,*
*some wounds deepen the*
*well that holds the water*
*that we drink of.*

Whether we want them to or not, our scars speak for us.

The stretch marks on the body of a mother. The road rash on the knees of a child.

The remnants of a surgical incision. The holes in the hands of a Savior.

Each of us carries experiences that have left us with stories. Some scars are visible, others hidden beneath the surface of our skin and spirit. But if we are willing to examine them with intention, we may uncover something beneath them—something deep, something sacred, something that was always meant to be offered to the world.

This is where I introduce you to Eugene Pauly.

Years ago, I came across his story when reading *The Power of Habit*. Eugene's life was forever altered by an unseen battle in his brain. Chronic encephalitis (inflammation of the active tissues in the brain) ravaged the part of his brain that dealt with memory and retention. The case was so extreme that it erased his ability to form new memories.

Eugene could not recall conversations from moments earlier in the day. He would prepare full meals, abandoning them in the kitchen while doing so. He couldn't recognize the new neighborhood he had moved into. And yet, in the midst of his madness and fading memory, the miraculous happened. Pre-illness, he practiced repetition—taking a walk each day around the block in his neighborhood. He'd done it for so long, he could do it with his eyes closed. And when his memory faded, his body remembered what his mind could not.

Even in all his forgetfulness, he was still faithful to his walk.

He would walk around his neighborhood daily, guided by an invisible yet ingrained sense of direction, always finding his way home. He could not explain how. He simply did it.[1]

His case fascinated neuroscientists because it revealed a profound truth: Habit is as strong as memory. The actions we repeat carve neural pathways, allowing us to operate even when conscious thought fails us.

Eugene's story became a metaphor for me—one that whispered, *What we do consistently, we become.*

*We are wired to adapt to what surrounds us.*

Then, years later, I stumbled upon Daniel Pauly and his research on *shifting baselines.*[2]

His work in marine biology sought to explain something that extended far beyond the ocean. He discovered that each generation unknowingly accepts a *diminished world* as their norm.

Over time, our perception of what is *normal* erodes, and we stop questioning losses that should have been unacceptable. We do not see the full scale of decline because we have only ever known the world as it exists *now.*

Pauly's findings were not just about the environment; they revealed something deeply human. *We are wired to adapt to what surrounds us* . . . and if we are not careful, we may unknowingly accept mediocrity, oppression, and the erosion of joy as simply "the way things are."

Two men. The same last name.

Two stories, seemingly unrelated.

But together, they taught me something profound:

We either live by the power of repetition or by the blindness of acceptance.

Some of us willingly accept reality as it is, neglecting the call to *activate our holy imagination.* We sit still, absorbing the world's foolishness as normal. We refuse to dig deeper, to fight against stagnation, to carve out a life that tells a different story.

But what if we charted a new path? What if we dared to *shape our stories with intention*, refusing to let life happen to us but instead choosing to be architects of a deeper, more meaningful existence? What if we didn't simply accept, but instead, we built?

A book, a film, a podcast, a poem, a wedding vow, a simple word spoken to a stranger—every expression of human creativity starts with an experience, often a scar.

A loss, a lesson, a moment of clarity. These experiences extend to us an invitation into the depth . . . the *tehom*.

The depth is often where the hardest truths reside. The depths of the sea hold the remnants of lost civilizations. The depths of our wounds hold the weight of stories we struggle to speak. And yet, just as God moved over the waters in the beginning, He moves over our deep places now—hovering, healing, calling forth light where there was once only darkness.

Maybe that's a question worth meditating on today.

Intentional time spent nursing your wounds could lead to healing—not just for yourself but for the world around you. Many of us have been taught to only look at our time, talents, or material resources as primary forms of offering to one another—but what if we sat for a second and considered that the undoing of misaligned things within our inner world was a form of offering and service to someone else too?

As we reflect on *tehom*, on wounds, and on what we carry within us, I leave you with this poem:

***If tomorrow didn't call my name . . . how***
***happy would I be?***
***How many places did I go? How many***
***people did I see?***

*How many moments filled with magic did*
*my eyes not get to see?*
*How many lost ones did I reach? How*
*many children did I feed?*
*. . . if contentment's in each moment, will*
*my joy ever reach its peak?*
*I find these questions in my mind before I*
*sigh and go to sleep.*
*I am afraid that if tomorrow called my*
*name, I'd pray it had mistaken me.*

Scars remind us of what we have survived. But urgency reminds us to live while we still can.

Don't be afraid to share your scars. They are the starting points of significance.

Shalom.

(سلام), Arabic, SAH-lahm

# 12 Salam

More than a hello, *salam* is a blessing spoken into being. It means "peace be upon you," but not peace as ease or silence. It is peace as wholeness. Completion. Rightness in the soul and among neighbors.

To say *salam* is to will the world well-being, to offer a spoken shelter, a wish for healing and harmony in the bones of a person's life. Rooted in the same soil as the word *shalom*, it carries the hope that all broken things might be made whole again—that in greeting another, we invoke the very possibility of restoration.

*Existing becomes easier*

*when we embrace*

*the art of absorbing*

*and expelling.*

As I've gotten older, my respect and acknowledgment of the need for therapy has grown in a dramatic fashion. As we're pushed into our silos and self-implemented isolation, there is prominent need for shared spaces that feel sacred and safe. As long as I've been going, therapy has always been that for me.

For starters, we all need uninterrupted environments to pause and process. Doing this with a trusted voice (who just so happens to be highly educated, licensed, and bound to confidentiality within those four walls) scratches many itches that sit on the skin of our human experience.

We get to be seen by someone, to be heard and acknowledged without interruption, and afforded the opportunity to confront any previous or present issues that may need processing.

I genuinely believe that speed and stimulation are the two things that keep us from intentionally slowing down to address our internal and external issues. This ultimately keeps us stuck in a loop, allowing life to become more exhausting than exhilarating.

It's no secret that our inputs are at an all-time high.

We're stimulated until we're senseless by glowing phone screens.

We get caught up in the constant consumption of mass media and nasty news cycles. We feed our biases by allowing the algorithms to inform us. We decline the call to think critically and connect our lives in community with others.

And in each action, we voluntarily assert ourselves into the fabric of this fallen world.

In this cultural moment, we feel everything, everywhere, all at once . . . both all around us and within us.

This act of *absorption* is a core tenet of human existence. We've always had inputs.

However, unprocessed absorption comes equipped with intrusive thoughts, overwhelming emotions, debilitating anxiety, and ultimately, subtle influences that shape our actions and keep us stuck in a loop.

On the other side of our absorption, however, exists the opportunity to *expel*.

To drop the emotional baggage and mental weight of yesterday. To refresh and renew our minds with great intention. To pause and process our greatest pains as well as the things that have positively impacted us. To be mindful of each minute that passes, realizing how connected it is to the next.

One of my favorite expressions is the insightful idiom: *It is what it is.*

I've noticed that sometimes we say words without wonder.

Certain expressions become so current in our cultures and communities that they sometimes lose their impact and importance, but the phrase *it is what it is* actually acts as an invitation into a raw reality.

Things were what they were, things are what they are, and the only influence we have over the future exists inside our honest acceptance about *what is happening right now.*

This doesn't mean denying any damage done; this doesn't mean forgetting and fumbling onto the next thing; this doesn't mean going numb and acting like something didn't happen. Instead, it means demonstrating faith, ushering in integrity, and accepting the courage needed to process life as it may be.

In the act of *absorbing*, we must also implement the art of *expelling*.

Expelling is incredibly difficult for me, because I am someone who has a high capacity for compassion and is emotionally influenced by empathy. These are beautiful benefits but can also be somewhat burdensome too.

A few summers ago, I ran into a dear friend while wrapping up an evening walk. We hadn't talked in a while—in fact, we'd been playing phone tag and missing each other quite frequently—but on this day we were destined to bump into one another.

We shared some niceties momentarily, but I could tell that there was something heavy on his heart. With compassionate curiosity and soft speech, I simply asked, "Are you okay?"

A few long moments passed, and he broke into tears.

I pulled him in and hugged him and let him cry as long as he needed to.

He shared how heavy life had become and gave a jarring nod to how dark his thoughts had been over the last week—overwhelming him to the extent that he expressed that "life felt too heavy to keep living"—and that the only thing keeping him from harm was his family, friend group, and the love of God.

On my ride home I began to pray for my friend, and at the end of the prayer I rode in silence—waiting in expectation for God to respond. The Holy Spirit ever so gently said to me: *You have absorbed this pain and emotion, but don't forget to that you need to* expel *it.*

Those are words that I desperately needed to hear . . . words we all need to hear today as we navigate the weight of our internal world, as well as the worlds that exist all around us.

It is respectful and responsible—both to God and to ourselves—to pause and process after we have emotionally charged or spiritually insightful experiences.

If we don't, we will walk through this life collecting weights from one another that we will carry longer than we have the time to—justifying our burdens and burnout under the guise of compassion and empathy.

My invitation to you today is to grieve, lament, pause, process, and pray. These are perpetual practices that will help us handle our humanity.

Stillness is what removes the weight of the burdens that we carry, acknowledging that God is above it all and able to meet us exactly where we are, with exactly what we need.

Shalom.

Italian, spret-tsa-TOO-ra

# 13 Sprezzatura

*Sprezzatura* is the grace of making it look easy—even when it isn't. It is the quiet confidence that comes from deep care, not performance. It's when someone moves through the world with such ease that you forget the hours, the hardship, the hidden labor behind it. But make no mistake—this isn't about perfection or pretending. It's about presence. Poise. The kind of mastery that doesn't need to announce itself.

To live with *sprezzatura* is to carry your calling lightly, not because it isn't heavy, but because you've learned how to hold it well. It's not arrogance. It's not apathy. It's the freedom that comes from doing your work with love and letting it speak for itself.

*Dreams jump from the heart,*

*desires rise from the eyes—*

*divinity exists within*

*the difference.*

For years, I wrestled with the idea of perfection. I held my work hostage in the waiting room of "not yet." I convinced myself that excellence required delay, that unfinished meant unworthy, that if I was patient enough, if I refined long enough, then one day I would create something worthy of release.

Then I met Jason.

Jason is one of my favorite humans, and maybe my favorite creative.

A poet, a filmmaker, a novelist. A curator of stories that linger long after they have been told. He moves through the world with an ease that is rare—every piece of art, every performance, every written word feels effortless, as if it emerged from him fully formed.

But one evening in October 2020, sitting on his couch, he unraveled the illusion. He told me about his early years as a songwriter—how, during his time in college, he had written *hundreds* of hymns for small Baptist churches across the country. He shared how many of those songs had never been heard outside the walls of his own mind.

And then, with the quiet weight of someone who had already learned what I had yet to understand, he said:

> Perfection is subjective, and the idea of perfection is the very enemy of the artist. If you wait until something is perfected to publish it, you will find yourself at the end of your life with more than just a hard drive filled with hundreds of songs—you will find yourself with dreams that didn't manifest and desires that died. And fear will be the reason you are unfulfilled.

On the drive home, my mind filled with the faces of artists who had shaped me. The authors whose words stitched me back together. The filmmakers whose stories pulled something sacred from my spirit. The poets who penned my pain to the page. The musicians whose melodies met me in moments of unraveling.

And I realized: Every piece of art that has ever healed me only exists because someone chose to release it before they thought it was perfect.

What if they hadn't?

If Dylan and Marley had kept their best songs hidden, they would have silenced generations longing for liberation. If Beyoncé had never recorded "Brown Skin Girl," millions of Black and brown girls might never have seen their beauty reflected back at them in song. If Martin Luther King Jr. had canceled his calling. If the poets had refused to pen. If the chefs had decided their craft was unworthy of the table. If the painters had never picked up their brushes.

How much of the world would be missing?

And yet, we convince ourselves that our gifts can wait. That what we carry is not necessary. That our words, our work, our wonder should be hidden until we deem them flawless. *We do not just take ease for granted—we treat it with suspicion.* We mistake effortlessness for insignificance, forgetting that our natural inclinations are not random—they are divine assignments.

*Sprezzatura* is the courage to create without the weight of perfection.

And it's not just about execution—it's about perception. It is what happens when skill becomes instinct, when the unseen hours of effort dissolve into a seamless display of ability. It is not about feigned indifference but rather a sacred surrender—an understanding that true excellence is found not in rigid control but in the willingness to let go.

We live in a world that often mistakes ease for entitlement. We assume that if something comes naturally to another, it must have cost them nothing. We overlook the weight of their unseen labor, the silent sacrifice beneath their success. And worse, we do this to ourselves—undervaluing the gifts that flow freely from us simply because they are effortless in our hands.

But ease is not an accident. It is an inheritance. A divine imprint. A gift meant to be given away.

It is the discipline of offering what we have, while we have it, in the state that it is in. It is understanding that the world is not made whole by what we hold back—it is healed by our giving away what we're holding.

In an episode of the show *Dark Matter*, a character named Amanda said:

> I used to think that life was about reaching some perfect destination.
>
> Because I hadn't reached it yet, I felt somehow ill at ease. But I had seen the perfection.
>
> I had reached it, and I'm starting to suspect that it is the imperfections of life that amount to a different kind of perfection.[1]

We chase after completion, thinking that only in its arrival will we find peace.

But what if the peace is in the pursuit? What if the imperfections—the *almosts*, the *not yets*—are not evidence of failure but proof of life?

This is the invitation—to embrace the fragments, to release what we have while we have it, to trust that what flows from us with ease is meant to be offered freely.

Think about the songs that steadied you in heartbreak. The film scene that gave language to your loneliness. The book that arrived like a friend when no one else understood. None of those moments happened by accident. They were offerings—imperfect, timely, deeply human.

We do not heal in isolation. We heal in the overflow of another's courage to share. To create is not just to express—it is to connect. Every gift released becomes a bridge, closing the distance between souls.

So my question is no longer *What if?*

It is: *What is?*

What is it that you are holding and hiding that you could be healing and handing to the world?

Because in the end, our becoming will not be marked by what we perfected but by what we *pursued in imperfection.*

Shalom.

(מִנְחָה), Hebrew, MEEN-khah

# 14 Minchah

*Minchah* is what you bring forward—not to impress, but to honor. In ancient tradition, it was the fruit of the land, the yield of your labor, laid bare before God. No blood, no barter—just bread, oil, and presence. It wasn't about *what* was given but *how*—with open hands, without demand, sometimes even without words.

*Minchah* is what we place before another when we've poured ourselves into something and release it anyway—not knowing if it will be held or overlooked. It's the beauty of offering without control. The faith to give something sacred without needing it to be understood. To live with *minchah* is to live from devotion, not transaction.

It is not payment. It is presence, extended.

*My heart turns from*

*empathy to apathy*

*when I extend my*

*hands to the world*

*and they would rather cuff*

*them than clap for me.*

I have always found it strange that the market gets to dictate and determine what is objectively successful when an artist or entrepreneur releases something special into the world.

People spend hours, days, weeks, and years (sometimes decades) turning their thoughts into actual things—only to reveal what they've been working on and it goes unacknowledged or unappreciated by the people they've prepared it for.

And sometimes that outcome and experience of being underwhelmed and unappreciated is the only income (for the artist) worth walking away with.

Somehow, we've slipped into a place as a society of swimming with the school of thought that seems the most attractive at the appointed time—we peruse comment sections on clickbait before we think critically; we'll trust the bias of the media before we build a narrative based on fact. We have a tendency to lean into entertainment more than we lean into the truth.

We're not always attracted to the ideas or innovators that hold the most wisdom, or the most substance, or even heal or offer what's helpful. Sometimes we just want what holds the most attention and affinity in the moment.

I wish I could say that this is by sheer happenstance, but dare I say—it's by design.

On one of my favorite podcasts, *The Minimalists*, cohost T.K. Coleman shared a quote that encapsulates the idea:

> Mark Zuckerberg once hired someone to investigate why some people were spending more time on Facebook than others. He later remarked: "The greatest minds of my generation are spending their

> thinking skills trying to figure out how to get people to spend more time online clicking on more advertisements."
>
> And we are so far from Athens. We are so far from the greatest minds of our time debating what it means to live the good life, or debating whether or not there's an objective morality, or debating whether or not there is a God, or debating biomedical ethics.
>
> The greatest minds of our time are debating: How can we get these folks clicking on more ads?
>
> And you even start to see it infecting philosophy, because even when there are philosophical debates, it's like we're all following some kind of script. We're all worried about the same things at the same time, because the algorithm says: "Hey, this is what everybody needs to be worried about now."[1]

This is humbling and horrifying all at the same time, because where we place our worth is where we build our worlds . . . and I'm afraid we either never learned or have forgotten how to follow the voices with vision.

We are in an era where highly intelligent individuals are incentivized to optimize user attention rather than to solve deeper societal issues. And personally, I get it—everything isn't for everybody. Contrary to popular belief, however, I do believe that everything is, in fact, *that deep.*

This is where the quintessential questions of *minchah* begin to emerge: Why do we give our attention to what our algorithms offer us, and why don't we push back against what is being presented? Additionally, what do we offer, and why? And more importantly: *Who do we allow to determine the value of what we create? Who do we let influence how we simply . . . exist?*

The constant tension between creator and consumer stems from the creator's longing for gratitude—and the consumer's power to withhold it.

We have been conditioned to believe that meaning is dictated by engagement metrics, that validation is measured in reactions, and that worth is determined by visibility.

*Minchah* reminds us otherwise. It tells us that offering—on either side—is an act of integrity, not performance. That the act of giving is a statement of independence—not from people, but from the false narratives that try to define success for us.

This is not just a commentary on technology; it's also about the dilution of independent thinking, the erosion of self-led exploration, and the loss of truly free thought. The algorithms that dictate attention have also dictated curiosity, flattening the expanse of possibility into a narrow, predetermined set of interests. And so we have become predictable. Clickable. Easier to categorize, easier to manipulate.

But what if we rejected that?

What if we reclaimed what it means to *seek* rather than simply *consume*?

What if we maintained our muses and explored our internal affinities?

What if we became untethered from the systems that tell us what matters and, instead, followed our own questions toward deeper, richer pursuits?

*Minchah* motions us toward the goodness of giving. It also highlights the significance of seeking.

You don't have to be a creative to live creatively. You just have to be willing to give what you have—even if it's not understood. Even if it's not clapped for. Even if it's not returned.

Because *minchah* is not measured by reception but by intention. It's not about how loud your gift is. It's about how true.

Sometimes the offering is your art. Sometimes the offering is your attention. Sometimes the offering is your apology.

Your entire life can be a liturgy. A lived expression of what matters most.

We exist in a time when algorithms compete for our affection, and attention spans are currency. And somewhere along the way, we started to believe that ease is more valuable than depth, that the path of least resistance is the path to purpose. But *minchah* calls us back to deliberate, defiant giving. Not just of our creations but of ourselves.

To live in full, radiant freedom—especially when the world withholds it—is a radical act of defiance.

Sometimes the world is wildly unfair and unfree.

And the only way to shake off those shackles is to let your life be the protest.

To live artfully. Audaciously. Honestly.

And I genuinely believe that rebellion that leads to redemption begins with self-respect.

The challenge today is to create the world you wish to see through the way you live your life—by seeking and making meaning as an act of resistance.

It's the call to swim against the current instead of being swept away in the school of collective distraction. It is the challenge to build something *real*, even if it is not *recognized*.

It is the demand to consume with intention and contribute your creation with devotion—not because the world demands it, but because *something in you knows it must be given*.

Shalom.

(בִּין), Hebrew, ben

# 15 Bîn

To understand, to perceive, to discern deeply within the mind.

In ancient Hebrew thought, *bîn* was not merely intellectual comprehension but an active engagement with wisdom. It was a seeing beyond what is immediately apparent, a perception that bridges emotions with truth. The root of the word is often linked to divine understanding—knowing beyond surface reactions, reading between the lines of human experience, and moving toward clarity.

The invitation of *bîn* is to live with discernment—to distinguish what feels true from what is true, to recognize emotions as guides rather than dictators. This kind of understanding requires a slowing down, a surrender to something beyond impulse, and a return to what is eternal and unshakable.

*God, please don't let the way that I feel get in the way of what's real.*

*No man can serve two masters, or so I have*
*been told.*
*My mind says trust in God, but my heart*
*says trust in gold.*
*A piece of me adores the world, and*
*everything that dwells within it.*
*But a totem spun still takes a fall,*
*no matter how you spin it.*
*So torn between the two within,*
*how could I ever choose?*
*An alarm of love rings from above,*
*somehow, I still hit snooze.*
*Just a few more minutes with the world, we*
*don't lie down that often . . .*
*yet the moves I make and the path I take,*
*could lead me to my coffin.*
*Afterlife stays on my mind . . .*
*how authentic could it be?*
*A set of angel wings for me . . . when I let*
*my demons lead?*
*I stand before my fate each day, not*
*knowing what I'll choose.*
*One gives a win, yet and still I sin . . .*
*my soul, it sings the blues.*

This is a poem that I wrote in 2017. It's entitled "A Soul Script." It not-so-subtly addresses the all-encompassing elements of the human experience, paralleled, of course, with spiritual life.

I used to feel so much shame as a child for simply . . . living.

Growing up in a Southern Baptist church, every Sunday was hell-fire and brimstone (I don't even know what brimstone is). It was "turn or burn" and "repent now for the coming of the Lord." It was no rap music or looking at women; it was no foul thoughts or emotions that made you feel the *dark parts* of your humanity. Fear-based teaching set the foundation for fear-based becoming.

Admittedly, even in my first encounter with the idea of salvation, I confessed my need for Jesus out of fear more than out of love. As I've gotten older, it's been one big act of undoing.

Having such a chaotic and confusing childhood, I felt pulled in so many different directions as an adult. I love hip-hop and R&B. I love cropping my clothes. I enjoy wearing short shorts to go on runs or hit the gym. I like making money and spending it. I enjoy sleeping in past my alarm and doing what I want with my day. I enjoy the sight of a beautiful woman. I cuss sometimes.

None of these things are evil or make me inherently unholy, but in my mind, there is a constant pinging conviction that holiness comes packaged only one way. I think a small percentage of it is the Holy Spirit, and a large percentage of it is my shame. Old voices vying for my energy and attention, reminding me that I'll never be as holy as I should be.

This has pushed me into the spiritual space of in-between. I don't feel like I fit into the neat Christian box the way I am expected to.

One part of my heart and mind is contemplative; the other part is charismatic. One part is understanding and empathetic; the other part is righteously indignant and offended at unholy ideas. One part is stern and serious; the other part thinks everything is a joke (and easily identifies the joke in everything).

In any honest spiritual journey, there comes not one, but many moments of revelation and need for reconciliation: when reading the Bible and finding things you don't agree with or things that are confusing. When hearing a word from a pastor whose sin you see and know, but they're shaming their audience as if they're spotless. When your lived reality is conversely contrasted from the prayers you've prayed and the progress you've pursued. When you find that God is gray.

While others may be drawn to the certainty of black and white, I have found that true understanding often lives in the tension of nuance. People in my past have tried to paint my spiritual journey in stark contrasts, but I have always known that subject matter with such depth requires a lifetime of experience and endless examination.

I know that my call is also to the culture. I serve as a bridge of translation between secular life and spiritual life—an intersection that I have inhabited for as long as I can remember.

My work is not about forcing conversion or assigning contingency to every conversation: It is about creating space for understanding.

I want to help those who have been hurt by the church or abused by authority see that God is still in His people, even when those who wave biblical banners fail to live by them.

Likewise, I want those who find themselves entrenched in secularism to know that they are not limited by the lifestyles they have succumbed to. I exist in the in-between, holding conversations that often go unheard, translating truths that many ignore.

But I know that this work comes at a cost. Holding this space—this responsibility—can be emotionally exhausting. I carry the weight of perspectives from all sides, seeking to honor both experience and truth. And in this tension, I am reminded of the importance of *bîn*—a deep discernment that anchors me in what is real beyond what is merely felt.

In psychology, *perceptual positions* refer to the ability to shift between perspectives—seeing a situation from multiple angles rather than being locked into one viewpoint.[1] It's a cognitive and emotional flexibility that allows for understanding beyond oneself. It is the mental posture required to engage with both sides of an argument, a belief system, or a worldview.

Most people live in one perceptual position. Some live only in their own convictions, others only see the pain of those around them, and others detach completely. But living in all three can be costly—this is why I feel the weight of the gray.

And when my work gets too heavy, I have to be reminded that I wasn't called to carry it alone and that God is my guide on the journey—making sense of the mess that black and white will always make.

And maybe you feel that weight too.

Maybe you're holding the tension of your own upbringing, your own beliefs, your own contradictions.

Maybe you're tired of the noise—of the headlines, the hashtags, the hot takes—and you're trying to figure out how to live in alignment with something deeper.

Let *bîn* be a mirror, not a measure.

Let it reflect what's real beneath the rush.

Let it hold space for the parts of you that don't fit neatly into categories.

*Bîn* reminds us that wisdom is not found in reaction but in discernment. It calls us to pause, to perceive, to separate emotion from truth—not dismissing emotion but allowing it to inform rather than control.

Perhaps *bîn* can help us see that we are not responsible for reconciling all things—only for standing faithfully in the tension.

So how do you engage with those you love—those who see the world differently than you do?

What might it look like to lead with understanding rather than assumption?

To ask deeper questions rather than offering quicker answers?

Connection rooted in *bîn* doesn't always mean agreement—it means presence.

It means choosing to stay in dialogue when silence feels safer.

It means holding space for nuance, even when clarity feels more comfortable.

It means embracing curiosity over critique.

Maybe this is why the prayer for our time together today is so essential: *God, please don't let the way that I feel get in the way of what's real.*

Because the exhaustion doesn't mean you are failing; it means you are deeply engaged in the work you were called to do. Maybe *bîn* calls you back to yourself. To your own rest. To your own divine clarity. To remind you that even God moves in the gray.

Emotions are best understood as indicators.

They are messengers, not masters.

When emotions come, let them enter, but do not let them define your reality. This is the ongoing work of staying anchored in your belovedness.

Shalom.

Swedish, YAHN-teh-LAH-gen

# 16 Jantelagen

A quiet code of conduct—not written in laws but lived in tone. *Jantelagen* is the unspoken agreement that says: Don't think you're better than anyone else. Rooted in Scandinavian culture, it values humility, collective responsibility, and the steady rhythm of shared life. It honors modesty, discourages grandstanding, and reminds us that belonging often begins where ego ends.

But *jantelagen* is not without tension. It can protect against arrogance, yes—but it can also stifle uniqueness, dimming the very light that was meant to be shared. It invites the question: How do we honor the whole without hiding the parts? To live with *jantelagen* is to walk the thin line between individuality and interdependence—to be fully yourself, but never at the expense of someone else.

*Perspective is important,*

*but so is position.*

We're all so afraid of dying, yet so few of us actually choose to live while we have the opportunity to do so.

Not in the *breathing, eating, working* sense—but in the full-bodied, soul-awake kind of way.

We scroll. We strive. We rehearse old wounds and future failures like they're scripts that deserve our devotion.

We call this vigilance when, in truth, it's disconnection. Somewhere between our survival instinct and our success addiction, we've forgotten how to live—and, perhaps more dangerously, how to enjoy what it means to be alive.

To receive a moment without rushing past it. To be known without performing. To tell the truth when someone asks, "How are you?" instead of opting out of honesty and into a conversation that has more to do with what you do.

This is the real threat of modern life: not death, but the slow erosion of presence.

And maybe this is what *jantelagen* was always quietly warning us against—not just arrogance or ambition, but the kind of self-centeredness that makes us believe we're separate from the fragile, fleeting rhythm of the world. That we're immune to the consequences of time, or too exceptional to be humbled. But even the great ones—those whose names echo through eternity—had to face the reality of this reckoning.

And none more vividly than Gilgamesh, whose story invites us to confront the myth of immortality, the illusion of control, and the cost of not being truly *here* while we still can be.[1]

The story of Gilgamesh is one of power, pursuit, and the weight of human mortality. He was a king, mighty and unmatched, a ruler with no equal. He believed in his own strength, his own legend, his own right to shape the world as he saw fit.

In his arrogance, Gilgamesh ruled with unchecked authority. His ambition knew no bounds; his name was whispered with both reverence and fear. He was the strongest, the most brilliant, the most cunning. He was the very definition of a man who did not believe in *jantelagen*—he saw himself above all, a force meant to be reckoned with, not humbled.

But he would learn after the tragic loss of a loved one that not even kings can outpace time.

Life would show him what strength alone could not conquer: loss.

When his closest companion, Enkidu, died, something inside Gilgamesh shattered.

The mortality he once ignored became his obsession. He set out on a desperate journey to defeat death itself, to find the secret to eternal life. He sought wisdom from the gods, from immortal beings, from forces beyond human comprehension. But the truth was simple and devastating: No man escapes time. None of us will make it out alive.

By the end of his life, Gilgamesh had power, but power was never the point. He had control, but control could not keep his life from slipping through his fingers. Only then, in the twilight of his reign, did he truly find humility.[2]

Only when he had everything did he realize he could not keep anything.

Gilgamesh was not the first man to learn this lesson late. His story echoes throughout history, reflected in kings, emperors, and leaders who built great kingdoms only to realize too late that their hands were never large enough to hold eternity.

Solomon had wisdom beyond measure, yet his desires led him astray (1 Kings 4:29; 11:1–4). Moses was called to lead, but he let frustration rob him of the promised land (Exodus 4:12; Numbers

20:8–12). Nebuchadnezzar stood atop his empire and declared his own greatness—only to be brought low until he acknowledged the sovereignty of God (Daniel 4:30, 33–34).

Time is the true hallmark of humility among humanity.

So often we forget, but we are all bound by time . . . so what we do with it and how we act will always be greater than what we accumulate and obtain while we're here.

Money and material are the invisible hand that often influence our actions . . . and if we're not careful, we'll continue to lower the bar of moral reasoning and exclude the necessities of life for the sake of meaningless material.

What we have will never make us who we are, but who we have and how we let Him work on our hearts always will.

Self-sufficiency seems attractive, but it is filled with fear and facade.

*Jantelagen* teaches that no one is above another, that collective strength matters more than individual ambition. But what happens when we resist this truth?

We build castles on sand. We chase power, thinking it will last.

We define ourselves by accomplishments rather than character.

We make new rules allowing us to reign over others as authorities.

Humility is not a loss—it is a foundation.

It is recognizing that perspective is important, but so is position.

That we can hold our humanity, but not forever.

That wisdom is not found in self-glory, but in knowing where we stand among others.

Gilgamesh thought he had time. So do we. But the question is: What will we do with the time we have? Will we chase a kingdom that cannot last, or will we learn the lesson before it is too late?

Here is a poem to ponder as we close our time together today:

*I won't be here long.*
*They won't sing my song.*
*They'll neglect my rights,*
*yet acknowledge my wrongs.*
*The quicksand will slip through the groove*
*in the glass*
*as I worship with work in the time that*
*will pass.*
*How I hope they'll remember the questions*
*I asked.*
*The love that I gave.*
*The prayers that I prayed.*
*The art that I offered,*
*the lives that I saved.*
*I've desired the most:*
*to feel seen and be known.*
*And to live in the gift*
*of the garden I've grown.*

Our lives are letters often read once they've been lived . . . so let the way you love shape a story worth reading.

Shalom.

( أنا بحبَك/ بحبِك ), Arabic, AH-nuh BAH-he-BACK

# 17 Ana Bahebak

In Christian theology, love is often understood as agape (unconditional, divine love).[1] The phrase *ana bahebak*, however, can take on a spiritual tone when used in faith-based contexts, reflecting the love of God toward humanity. Arabic translations of the Bible often use the word *macḥabba* (ةبحم) when describing God's love, but the sentiment behind *ana bahebak* can still echo a deep, self-giving love.[2]

Arabic culture, deeply rooted in tribal and communal identity, sees love as more than just romantic—it is familial, communal, and even covenantal. Love in this sense is tied to belonging and responsibility. When used in spiritual or interpersonal contexts, it can express a love that says, "I see you. I choose you. I stand with you."

*You can hold your tongue*

*but you cannot hold*

*your heart.*

Justice, as the world defines it, is often transactional—a wrong repaid, a debt settled, a punishment assigned. The system demands repayment as a means of restoration. But biblical justice is not only about *reparation*; it is also about *restoration*.

To clothe the naked, feed the hungry, shelter the unhoused, and care for those on the margins is not an act of pity—it is an act of worship. It is glorifying to God to restore humanity *because it is right*, not because it is owed.

One of the clearest examples we see of this idea is silently displayed in Mark 10.

Blind Bartimaeus sat on the margins, shunned and forgotten. The rich young ruler stood at the center, admired and secure. Their stories, placed in the same chapter, are no accident—they are a contrast of love, generosity, and justice in action.

Both men encountered Jesus. Both had an *ana bahebak* moment—Jesus loved them, but His love called them forward. Their responses define the difference between possession and surrender, security and faith, clinging and letting go.

The rich young ruler was hiding his hand while talking to Jesus; he wanted to know how to inherit eternal life. He walked up on Jesus with sweet words. He recalled his past and championed his own childhood as perfection. He stood in confidence and curiosity, asking the most potent question he could—only to receive the last thing that someone in his shoes wanted to hear. Jesus replied to him, "Go sell everything you own. Give the money to the poor, and you will have riches in heaven. Then come with me" (v. 21 CEV).

That man fell to his knees, then walked away in woes.

In the most powerful moment of his life's existence, he wasn't willing to loosen his grip on his means or material things—showing where his heart was, even though he came *empty-handed.*

Blind Bartimaeus, on the other hand, had a radically different experience—changing his earthly existence and his eternal one too.

He shouted for Jesus despite being told to be silent. His love is undignified, desperate, unafraid of rejection. The crowd told him to stay quiet; he got louder. Jesus called him. Bartimaeus threw off his coat—his only possession—and ran toward Jesus. His faith, not his status, made him whole. He asked for sight, and Jesus gave it freely.

Unlike the rich young ruler, Bartimaeus followed.

Everything costs someone something. *Everything.*

And sometimes, you will find that the life God is calling you into will almost always cost you the one the world convinced you to settle for.

There are prayers that we can't pray, ideas we can't access, emotions we can't express—unless we're willing to negotiate new normals on life.

And the new normals we need to negotiate can be captured in our ideas and orientation toward generosity and justice. The ways we choose to say we see people, how we champion others and choose them, how we untie the knots the world has tied—repairing and restoring the wrongs.

There are versions of ourselves waiting for us in the future, beckoning us to belong—versions of us who idealize and embody the beauty of biblical love. Love that opposes and inverts worldly ideas and lives counterculturally, calling others into all that they can be.

Love—*ana bahebak*—is a holy disruption.

It demands a shift in posture, a loosening of grip, a reorientation of the heart. Justice and generosity are not optional add-ons to faith; they are the essence of faith itself.

If we are to truly embody the love of Christ, we must understand that love is not just felt; it is given, restored, and lived. It is also easily visible to those who long for it the most.

The rich young ruler teaches us that holding tightly to what we possess may leave us empty. Bartimaeus teaches us that surrendering all we have may lead us to wholeness. The question remains: *Will we love in a way that repairs, restores, and reshapes the world?*

Maybe the answer isn't found in a declaration but in a decision—the quiet kind we make in real time, in traffic, in tension, in the middle of tired conversations.

Maybe love looks less like a grand statement and more like a daily return to generosity, to justice, to joy. Because even if the world doesn't shift overnight, something in us will.

And maybe that's where the real reshaping begins.

We can hide our hands, but we can't hide our hearts. How we act—and what intentions influence us—will ultimately hold the answer.

Shalom.

Portuguese, saa-DAH-jee

# 18 Saudade

*Saudade* refers to the presence of absence—taking a melancholic delight in what is gone. Though akin to nostalgia or longing, the term has no direct equivalent in English.[1]

A haunting ache for something lost, or perhaps never fully had. *Saudade* is the sweet ache of remembering—a longing not just for a person, place, or time, but for the feeling they once evoked. It is the presence of absence made tender, where memory and desire converge in a soft, sorrowful light. Unlike nostalgia, which romanticizes the past, *saudade* holds space for its ache, allowing beauty and grief to sit at the same table. It is a love that endures even in absence, a melody hummed to a silence that once sang back.

*Desires are often created within our deepest deficits.*

The idea of *imago Dei* has always been so fascinating to me.

In the expression of our individuality, we get to see a great big God give the gift of generosity—breaking off pieces of Himself and issuing them to everyone who has ever lived.

When we look into the mirror, however, I wonder how many of us appreciate and acknowledge that we are so much more than what we see. Every label that we've ever lived under, every idea that we've given emotion to, every experience that we've ever endured, everything that we've ever believed about ourselves—be it true or false—I genuinely wonder if we have ever *honestly* expressed (and agreed) that we were created in the image of God?

I wonder if we have ever truly realized that the God of heaven and earth had us in mind at creation, that He saw it fit to give us this one little life. That this God desired to behold the nuance of our humanity, our ethnic makeup, our culture and all its expressions, our ideas and emotions, gifts and good works. All these things are inherently divine and instilled with worth before the world put its words on us and attempted to alienate us from our eternal identity.

The hard truth about accepting this idea is that our ideas of ourselves (rooted in insecurity, pride, prejudice, or programming) all fall short when hung beneath the banner of heaven.

Embracing our divinity requires humility from our humanity.

It requires us being honest with ourselves about the things we've let influence our idea of individuality, learning how to loosely love the things that have brought us life and let go of the hindrances that have not.

Personally, I still face a daily struggle in simply accepting the fact that I am a beloved son.

I place pressure on myself and hold the unnecessary tension of believing that my performance and progress are somehow the things that please God the most, and yet holding tight to the competing truth that *simply existing* is enough.

It seems like somewhat of a constant struggle between striving and stillness.

Striving—stemming from feeling or being unseen, a real wrestle with inherent self-worth—builds a boldness within someone that ultimately evolves into survival. Personally and professionally, striving sets the standard of what feels sufficient—in your work, in your love life, in your faith journey. Always fighting forward until what you've achieved allows you to feel like you've arrived at *your idea* of enough.

Stillness, on the other hand, is the antithesis of striving and survival. It's internal order, the place of peace that cannot be irritated by external issues. Stillness makes us less prone to chaos and the culture that comes equipped with it. Stillness gives you time to evaluate the truth of fact before you run off toward the fault line of your fleeting feelings—setting a pace in the race that only someone in survival can run.

I wonder which side you're on today: on the side of striving and surviving, or sitting in the satisfaction slowly stirred up through stillness?

*Saudade*, our word for today, shines a light on the significance of both sides.

The echoing ache for something lost, or perhaps never fully had. *Saudade* brings a reverence to remembering—a longing not just for a person, place, or time but for the feeling they once evoked.

Maybe today you're after a version of yourself that feels familiar. Maybe you're chasing an image that you've created in your mind that upholds an identity that feels like it's enough—to you. Maybe you're lamenting a picture from the past that holds the heart of who you think you are.

Wherever you are, whoever you are, I want to express the urgency and importance of understanding your identity, because who we are inspires what we want.

Remember: Our desires are often created within our deepest deficits.

And the only way to dig up the root of those deficits is to turn inward and explore—to get acquainted with old versions of ourselves that have helped craft the inner workings of our identity.

This is a cornerstone of cognitive behavioral therapy—specifically, inner-child healing.[2]

If you're unfamiliar, many clinicians and practitioners create a safe space for you to explore what's going on inside you, often inviting you to revisit vivid memories, describing your emotional state or examining the aftermath of events that occurred earlier in your life.

This practice acts as protection for your adulthood decision-making, prompting you over time to understand your reactions or responses based on what events you experienced at younger ages of life.

If you were bullied as a child, any sense of domineering authority may be triggering for you.

Did you grow up in a toxic home environment with verbal aggression or abuse? If so, you're probably exceptionally sensitive to the ongoings of an argument. Maybe you're overwhelmed by affirmation and don't take compliments well (although you deserve them) because you didn't get them enough when you were younger.

It's astounding how much of adulthood is an echo of early experiences.

The healed and unhealed parts of us show up daily—either acting from what we have in abundance or aching for what we lack.

This is why we have to carry a watchful sense over what we want for.

Maybe it's your affinity for achievement.

Maybe it's your journey toward justice.

Maybe it's your itch for intimacy.

Maybe it's your anger aimed at inequality.

Only *you* know *your* affinities and agitations.

However, the beauty of your individual experience exists in how you apply your creative best toward the deficits that live deep within you.

In the presence of absence, we must pause and ask why we want what we want before we begin walking toward it.

Shalom.

(μετάνοια), Greek, meh-a-NOY-uh

# 19 Metanoia

Meaning a significant change of heart and mind, often occurring in one who repents.

Experiencing a subsequent, positive psychological rebuilding or healing.[1]

A holy undoing, *metanoia* speaks to the deep and inward turning—a profound shift of heart, mind, and direction, often born from sorrow but marked by grace. It is not just repentance but reorientation, a falling apart that makes room for truer wholeness. The soul's tectonic shift toward alignment, toward light, toward life. *Metanoia* is the unseen work beneath transformation—the moment when a person, faced with truth, chooses healing over hiding. It is the doorway between who we were and who we're becoming.

*Help me prune my foolish pride*

*help me expose,*

*instead of hide*

*this very privileged*

*life of mine,*

*the very one I've idolized.*

*Why does it pain you*
*that I can raise my voice*
*without moving my lips?*
*That I can make time stop*
*with a singular thought*
*and with nothing more than motion*
*I can make magic.*
*That society makes me antsy*
*and prerequisites never fit my fancy.*
*Even the most beautiful boxes can cause*
*my claustrophobia to increase.*
*That's why*
*I need my space, man.*
*I won't shake not one more hand*
*make one more plan*
*or two-step to one more song*
*or dance.*
*In my mind, I've redefined romance*
*and there's just enough room for two.*
*Odds are I'd take two of me*
*over three of you.*
*I'm not always strong:*
*I still long for love.*
*I have a sensitive side*
*And I have never been too tough.*
*I like black coffee in my cup*
*and my whiskey neat, and strong.*
*No matter what tomorrow brings*
*I must sit still and tune my strings*

*I'm out of rhythm*
*When I'm made to get along.*
*I need my solitude:*
*that's where I sing my song.*

This is a poem from my first book, *Humanity's Table*. It's titled "I Became an Introvert at 25."

And although you may laugh at the title, it is not an exaggeration.

The first twenty-five years of my life were spent gaining energy and excitement from the company of companions, family, and friends—an extrovert's extrovert, if you will. But after working in entertainment for four straight years, stepping on stages, rocking microphones, and controlling crowds, I found myself extremely exhausted after long days on the road, often managing overwhelming events.

The switch being flipped wasn't necessarily about people, though; I genuinely do love people, being around them, sharing and hearing stories. It had more to do with the amount of work, obligations, and atmosphere I was constantly exposed to. Over time, the slow drip of draining happened, and my social battery seemed to always be on empty.

My capacity to care had gone cold.

Work would end but my day wasn't over.

I tried to sleep but couldn't turn my mind off.

Stimulation invaded my silence.

All I ever wanted was solitude.

My desire for rhythms of rest and relaxation began to take precedence over people.

My days of solitude and silence began to occupy my agenda more than anything else.

Outside of my work, I had longed for a life of leisure, and over time I had achieved it.

I had come to realize, however, that comfort was costly. I accepted that my life of leisure and solitude was more important than my obligation to keep my capacity available to the heart of humanity. That no story was too small to sit with. That no issue affecting a world away from mine was too minuscule to spend minutes meditating on.

So I began to pray this prayer:

*Help me prune my foolish pride*
*help me expose, instead of hide*
*this very privileged life of mine,*
*the very one I've idolized.*

This prayer came from a place of impatience and perspective. It often finds its way to the surface when I'm too comfortable, tucked away in my little corner of the world. When I've silenced ongoing situations and scenarios separate from my own. When my prayers and pursuits are self-centric. When my awareness is numbed to the obligations of others.

When I'm less proximate to people . . . on purpose.

Although I do believe that comfort can be a *blessing* that flourishes from blood, sweat, and tears, it can also act as a *burden* to those who innocently allow their comfort to turn into a form of control.

It often happens unknowingly too.

A swipe here, another episode there, another meal here, an extra coffee there.

Canceling on this friend, ending an obligation early, staying up late to scroll.

We may not realize it, but many of us have curated our worlds with comfort as our center. And if we're not carefully aware of how we continue, we can let our daily routines deepen our program of privilege—a pattern that prioritizes self over surrender, turns its nose up at sacrifice, and neglects the duty of loving one's neighbor.

Becoming proximate to people is the thing that changes us.

We need people who don't think like us, vote like us, act like us, believe like us, or perceive the same way that we do. We need new ideas and new opinions. We need to be challenged by change.

Distance is dangerous. It's the thing that allows apathy to creep in and capture our hearts, desensitizing us to the evils of the world and the outlook of others.

Distance bakes the cake and cuts no one else a slice.

And if we're always standing afar in our ivory towers, looking down on others in distress, we'll fail to leverage our lives in a loving, compassionate, and careful way.

The call today is to not let your comfort keep you from caring about the issues that others face, because if the experience were your own, you'd want empathy too.

After all, space is sacred, so holding it for yourself first, and learning how to increase your capacity to offer it to others, is sometimes the most honoring thing that you can do.

If you're someone who struggles with overstimulation and the need for solitude, know that your *no* is just as powerful as your *yes*, and when you use both answers intentionally to any invitation, the shared space between yourself and someone else becomes even more sacred.

Shalom.

(שָׁלוֹם), Hebrew, sha-LOHM

# 20 Shalom

Not simply "peace"—*shalom* is the sound of everything in its rightful place. It is wholeness embodied. Integrity restored. A state where nothing is missing, and nothing is broken. More than the absence of conflict, *shalom* is the presence of alignment—within the self, among neighbors, and before God. It is when your inner world no longer fractures under the weight of performance, and your outer life becomes an echo of the harmony within.

*Shalom* speaks to integration—where mind, body, spirit, and story are not at war but at rest together. It is when your soul stops clenching and your presence becomes safe—for yourself, and for others. It is personal, yes, but never private. It extends outward, insisting that justice, reconciliation, and repair are not optional but essential. That to pursue *shalom* is to become a living answer to someone else's ache.

It is the garden before the fall, and the restoration after. The promise that healing is not only possible—it is holy.

*Living wholly*

*is a byproduct*

*of living holy.*

There is something unsettling about the way we engage with anything that doesn't speak our first language. We hear words, see shows, listen to music, and experience art through the lens of the language(s) that we understand . . . and the less we comprehend, the more curious we should become. But instead of curiosity, we often critique. Instead of wonder, we withdraw. Instead of asking what we might be missing, we dismiss it altogether.

Kendrick Lamar's halftime performance at the 2025 Super Bowl was an electrifying display of lyricism, movement, and cultural symbolism—a master class in storytelling. Yet, it was met with sharp criticism from those who found it uncomfortable or incomprehensible.

The issue that I've found is that we often don't stop to ask the question: What if our inability to understand isn't a failure of the artist but a failure of the audience?

Instead of reckoning with the message and imagery, people got stuck on the surface.

The sound mix. The song choice. The stage.

The performance wasn't the problem—the refusal to engage in understanding was.

A friend, also processing the performance, reached out to me later in the night and asked a simple but striking question: "Do you think the burden of connection is on the artist presenting the art, or on the receiver engaging with it?"

And immediately, I thought about Bad Bunny.

The album he released in 2025, *DeBÍ TiRAR MáS FOToS*, is a masterpiece, and yet, for the non-Spanish speaker, it may feel like a locked door.[1] However, the keys that open that door present themselves through curiosity. Although I'm over six hundred days in on my

Duolingo streak, and many Spanish-speaking lessons later—I can still only comprehend about half of what he's saying on the album.

Benito Antonio—the artist behind Bad Bunny—is responsible for telling his story and offering his art as an authentic expression of culture, struggle, and sound. But it is on me (as the *listener*) to take on the responsibility of attempting to approach more understanding.

If I don't do that . . . this is where *shalom* is fractured.

This type of fracture happens within us when we chase identities that are externally dictated rather than internally cultivated.

It happens within communities when cultures are erased, ignored, or misunderstood. It happens within nations when people are divided by race, ethnicity, and ideology—relegated to silos that strip them of connection and understanding.

We have been conditioned to see personal preference as an entitlement, as if our understanding should always be prioritized. When we refuse to engage with cultures outside our own, we don't just reject the art—we reject the people.

The privilege of never having to stretch beyond what is familiar robs us of the very connections that make us whole as humans.

Imagine society as a pie, with resources controlled by a select few who exclude others who also contributed to its creation. The berries came from a Black farmer. The flour was harvested from Indigenous land. The hardware it was cooked in was created by a Ghanaian in a glass factory. The stove itself was designed by Asian appliance artisans. And yet, the ones who own the stove and cook the pie get to decide who does and doesn't get a slice.

This is the American condition: the tension of *who belongs* and *who is excluded*. The false belief that one cultural expression is the standard by which all others are measured. It is a system of control, wrapped in nationalism and individualism, designed to silence rather than seek understanding.

Everything about Kendrick's performance was inherently American.

He exercised his freedom of speech.

He stood on his story.

He had the freedom to be unapologetically himself.

And yet, his art was dismissed as *other*. Too unfamiliar. Too uncomfortable. The refusal to engage wasn't about clarity—it was about *comfort*.

This is why *shalom* is not just an inner peace but an *active* one.

It is impossible to pursue *shalom* while rejecting the fullness of another's humanity. If *shalom* is completeness, then cultural supremacy—this idea that our experience, language, and worldview should be centered—is its greatest enemy. It is impossible to claim peace while ignoring the fractures we refuse to mend.

Theologically, *shalom* calls for an embodied peace—one that moves beyond tolerance into deep appreciation. The gospel compels us to see people not as "other" but as *image bearers of God. Imago Dei*—the divine imprint on every human life—means that wholeness is not complete until it is shared.

This is why racial reconciliation is not an optional pursuit for the believer but an essential one. It is not about diversity for diversity's sake; it is about embodying the kingdom.

What if we approached unfamiliar art—not just Kendrick's performance, but every expression of culture that does not fit neatly into our own experiences—with *a posture of humility rather than dismissal*?

What if we saw every language, every rhythm, every perspective as an opportunity to expand rather than a threat to defend against?

Because *shalom*—true, embodied *shalom*—demands this of us.

It is only realized when we embrace the fullness of humanity, both within ourselves and in others. To be whole, we must acknowledge and appreciate the richness of our own identities while extending that same honor to those who are different from us. This is not just a social necessity—it is a spiritual mandate.

I've said it before and I will say it again until the end of time: One day, we will ultimately learn in one way or another that *our differences do not make us dangerous—they make us divine.*

Shalom.

# 02 External Connection

(φιλότιμο), Greek, fee-loh-TEE-moh

# 21 Philotimo

*Philotimo* describes an attitude toward oneself, one's neighbors, and humanity at large. It means showing empathy, compassion, and generosity without expecting anything in return—taking pride in doing what is right and honorable while being humble at the same time.

The quiet dignity of the soul made visible in action, *philotimo* is a way of being—a deep inner compass that directs one toward honor, generosity, and love for others without asking for applause. It is the sacred sense of responsibility to do what is right, even when no one sees.

More than pride or virtue, *philotimo* is the invisible thread that binds community together, rooted in respect, selflessness, and the relentless desire to live with integrity. To have *philotimo* is to carry the weight of goodness as if it were joy.

*Your humanity is*

*a gift from heaven*

*that can help*

*heal the world.*

Your humanity is a gift from heaven that can help heal the world.

Many of us have been sold the antithesis of this truth, falling victim to disappointment, dissatisfaction, and shame. But this unique, one-of-one creation that you are exists *on purpose* and *for purpose*. There is digging required, however, to unearth all that you are.

This was revealed to me year after year after leaving my home state of West Virginia and moving to Atlanta, Georgia. I met mentor after mentor, artist after artist, and teacher after teacher whose stories resembled bits and pieces of my own.

Each interaction was a mirror moment, silently showing me who I was capable of becoming. The noticeable difference between myself and those mentioned, however, was how intimately these individuals understood themselves, and how freely they shared their stories. There was a subtle safety in how each person expressed themselves—with honesty, integrity, and transparency—a presentation that was proof positive because of the depths they had to dig before their discovery.

Have you ever met someone so certain of themselves that they're absolutely unshaken by anything that affected them earlier in their life?

The depths of their despair do not weigh them down, and at the same time, they're modest when mentioning any paramount moment experienced on the pathway to discovering their purpose.

The scales of justice in their life show as success on one side and shame on the other, and somehow they have subtly removed the sting from both.

They know the power of their potential, but they also know the shadows that sit within themselves just as well.

These extremes harken proximity to humility.

I've learned that the virtue of *humility* and the experience of *humiliation* are oddly interconnected.

Both words come from the Latin word *humus*, meaning "earth" or "ground."[1] One word speaks to a spirit that is grounded; the other speaks to the experience of being brought low.

True humility is rarely an inherent trait that we're born with . . . but is often birthed by being buried by the avalanche of life—the struggle of coming back up to the surface, stripping away the ego, and reminding us that we are literally *dust*.

If there is no burden to bear, we will always be defeated by friction. If there's no adversary to stave off, we never discover the extent of our strength. If there's no discontent or disappointment, we're never implored to discover.

Humiliation may break us, but it's also how hardened hearts become softened, making space for empathy, compassion, the sweetness of story, and an understanding of self that is only taught by receiving the grace of God.

This is how you share from a place of certainty and not places of insecurity.

This is how you embrace abundance and fight off living from fear.

This is how you appreciate where you come from, even when your environment alienated you.

This is how you appreciate the parent who wasn't present in your life during your childhood.

This is how you remove the sting of shame from an experience you never invited into your life.

This is how you remain humble after traversing the valley and making it to the mountaintop.

It's the humility, birthed from hardship (and what feels like humiliation), that develops a character within us that longs to continue.

Let me remind you again:

***Your humanity is a gift from heaven that can help heal the world.***

When we're numb, we have to come back to knowing.

When we're underwhelmed, we have to observe the extraordinary.

When we've become accustomed to bias, we have to come back to *beholding*.

What if today you practiced what it meant to *behold*?

*Beholding* is the archaic act of observing, paying close attention to, and admiring something or someone.[2]

Beholding often occurs when an object is revered as remarkable, when eyes and attention are earned.

And this practice of beholding today may offer you the ability to honor who you are for the first time in a long time. Tapping into the truth that your humanity can bring beauty to the brokenness of this world, but that it requires you to be bold enough to behold *who you are*.

Not what has been said about you, not your job title, financial status, where or who you come from, your wounds, or even the words that have been weaponized against you. With no filter or focus on all things external, *who are you at your core?*

This is a question that can only be answered when you take the time to consider how you have been crafted; answers arrive when you take the time to ask and you eagerly await their arrival.

The world is in need of your unique identity: Your perspective is powerful. Your ideas are eclectic. Your pains and proclivities are important. Your gifts are genuine and your skillset can be a catalyst for courage. Your emotions are indicators of expression. Your creative ingenuity is infinite. Your traumas can become instruments of momentum.

All of it—when examined and appreciated, upheld, and made whole—can act as a road map toward redemption. There's never been a better time to be yourself, bent toward good, offering what you can and who you are to others with compassion and care.

Shalom.

(تراضين), Arabic, TAH-ra-deen

# 22 Taarradhin

This phrase describes a way of reconciliation, where both sides win. A collective compromise, where everyone is more than happy with the outcome. The sacred art of mutual peace.

*Taarradhin* is not simply compromise; it is the rare and holy meeting point where hearts align without one having to lose for the other to win. A kind of reconciliation that leaves no residue of resentment, only the fullness of understanding.

It is the outcome of listening deeply, of honoring dignity on both sides. *Taarradhin* is when justice wears a human face—where mercy and fairness dance in balance, and all parties walk away whole. It is peace with a pulse.

*People are asking*

*earthly questions*

*that require*

*eternal answers.*

It's happening every day, all around us.

Some call it an existential crisis. Others call it mere curiosity. Some ignore it or don't know how to identify it at all—but by way of thought, feeling, or experience, people are asking earthly questions that require eternal answers.

Those who live a more earthly oriented lifestyle believe that they have the solutions to these existential issues. In another camp, closer than one could comprehend, there are those who are tapped into a more eternal viewpoint, operating from a much more spiritually inclined standpoint.

There are great arguments and ideas on both sides of the aisle, but I don't think the question is: Who is right? I think the real question is: How do the two camps respect the resolutions and find a holistic way to meet in the middle?

Less lashing out, more listening.

Less preaching and prescribing, more praying and pursuing.

Less demanding and damning, more dealing in empathy and intention.

Today's word, *taarradhin*, has a solution and pathway forward for any and all opposing sides. It speaks to a kind of reconciliation where both sides win. A collective compromise that leaves everyone more than content. It's not about the defeat of one side or the triumph of another.

It's about healing what's broken through shared understanding and creative contribution.

Throughout history, some of the most profound acts of *taarradhin* have come not from those in power but from those who were oppressed.

In America, one of the greatest examples of this is the creation of the blues.

During the horrific era of slavery, African Americans, stripped of almost everything—freedom, dignity, family—gave the world a gift so priceless that it continues to resonate through every corner of modern music. As one of my favorite authors, Kurt Vonnegut, once observed, nearly all popular music today—jazz, swing, rock-and-roll, hip-hop—can trace its roots back to the blues.[1]

But the blues wasn't just music. It was a way of surviving. A way of shooing away despair. A remedy for sorrow that could push depression into the corners of any room where it was played.

The irony, as noted by the great jazz historian Albert Murray, is that during slavery, the suicide rate among slave owners was far higher than among the enslaved.[2] The oppressors, despite their power and material wealth, succumbed to despair. Meanwhile, those who had every reason to give up found a way to sing and share stories through their suffering. They didn't just endure—they created.

This is the heart of *taarradhin*. Instead of choosing destruction, they chose creation. Instead of allowing their stories to be silenced by oppression, they filled the air with music—stories of pain, yes, but also of resilience, hope, and humanity. The blues became a way to reconcile unbearable sorrow with the need to keep living.

There's something deeply sacred about that choice. And it's a choice available to each of us today. The world doesn't need more destruction, more division, more unchecked, individualistic rebellion.

What it needs is people who are willing to bring healing to broken spaces—people who take what they've experienced and transform it into something that invites others into reconciliation.

*Taarradhin* calls us to create where we *could* destroy. To reconcile where we *could* retaliate. To find ways of leading with love in the midst of loss.

This is the art of joyful rebellion—choosing to create impactful revelation through an unconventional lens of love. This can look like many things: Writing a poem about the problem and sharing it with the world. Creating a soft space for listening in an overly loud location. Leaning into discomfort and speaking truth to power when you're outnumbered and overwhelmed. Putting your mood into a melody that softens the hardest hearts and invites us to find common ground.

Enslaved Africans taught us that even in the face of immense suffering, we can create something beautiful, something healing, something that reconciles.

The challenge for us today is to do the same—to take our stories, our pain, our experiences, and offer them to the world as acts of reconciliation through our joyful rebellion.

Your life—led with love—could be an invitation into the answer that someone's soul is searching for.

Today, I pray you stoke the fire of your holy imagination and find a way to somehow share.

Shalom.

German, SHA-den-froy-duh

# 23 Schadenfreude

The unsettling thrill of someone else's stumble. *Schadenfreude* is the strange flicker of satisfaction we feel when misfortune befalls another—a mirror held to our own insecurity, masked as amusement. It is not hatred but proximity. The subtle relief that we are not the one failing, faltering, or falling behind.

In a culture built on comparison, *Schadenfreude* exposes the fragile corners of our own self-worth. To name it is not to endorse it, but to recognize its shadow—and perhaps, in doing so, to choose compassion instead.

*Words are weapons,*

*be careful what you wield.*

The further away I walked from religion, the more cared for I felt in my communion with God.

This is an expression I used to feel uncomfortable sharing, until I realized how significant it was to the truth of my story (and the stories of many others).

I grew up in southern West Virginia, a place often referred to as "Wild and Wonderful."

Mountain ranges as far as the eye can see, rolling hills of green, fall foliage that feels like it's in 4K, blue skies, and wonderful weather. Kindhearted humans, Southern charm, and tight-knit communities that come from coal towns, hills, and hollers.

This place was the soil that my spiritual seed fell on.

My church experience as a child was diverse and very different. I come from a family who values God and the strength that spirituality brings, so we were often at the church when the doors were open. Sunday service (of course), choir practice, mime and drama club, and vacation Bible school. We made the rounds. When I say "if the doors were open, we were in attendance," I mean that.

My home church was of the Southern Baptist denomination. We sat in pew seats handcrafted of hardwood; we held weathered hymnals to sing our songs, lifted our hands as we worshiped, patiently passed the collection plate, took Communion together, and sat next to one another in a sanctuary filled with light that crept in through the sacred stained glass windows.

This church was where I learned about Jesus.

I learned about the importance of the Old Testament, and how it held hands with the gospel.

This is where I was taught the Ten Commandments. Where I learned about the disciples. The Pharisees. Adam and Eve. Moses. Noah and the ark. Ruth and Boaz. Saul. The apostle Paul.

David and Bathsheba. From front to back, and back to front, I became a believer in that Book.

The biblical knowledge brought forth by this church laid the foundation for my faith, and for that I will forever be grateful.

But as I look back, admiring my faith and how it has flourished, I can't help but address the agony and shame assigned to me by the same people who helped build my belief.

It's a dichotomy that is not divine.

I've struggled with shame for more than half of my life, and as I've worked through the many hurdles of healing, I can honestly say that most of my shame comes from the connection made by the "people of God"—for me—about the principles of God.

The same people who told me to correct my character and assess my sin also made me feel shameful about the color of my skin.

This was the place where I learned love on contingency. The cross that Christ died on for my sins was sufficient for all people, but all people weren't looked at as equal.

The words of God were weighty, assigning my inherent worth (or lack thereof) until I accepted much later in life that those who represent God sometimes rewrite His language and misrepresent His intentions.

This was the place where I learned what it meant to lament.

If this was the way that I was being treated as a partitioner and contributor to the church—one of God's people—I couldn't help but consider the place and pain of the people who had a longing for the love of God and the healing that comes from His heart, but only received reprimand and a hurtful hand of rejection when attempting to come close to the cross.

This is why I say:

***Words are weapons, be careful what you wield.***

The pivotal point for me in my journey with shame came from releasing the words that I agreed with that were placed upon me by people with ill intent. I accepted my obligation to undo what was done to me.

I had allowed people who had no interest in sitting with my story and letting me share to speak into it, infiltrating its most intimate part with words that withered my worth.

After years of asking God why my experience was what it was, I was handed an answer.

> Blessed be the God and Father of our Lord Jesus Christ, the Father of mercies and God of all comfort, who comforts us in all our affliction, so that we may be able to comfort those who are in any affliction, with the comfort with which we ourselves are comforted by God. For as we share abundantly in Christ's sufferings, so through Christ we share abundantly in comfort too. (2 Corinthians 1:3–5 ESV)

What falls upon you in life isn't always for you.

Sometimes the lessons you learn are meant for you to lend to others while they're lamenting too.

I genuinely believe that parts of our journey are so excruciating at times so that we can give away to others (in need) what we wish we'd had when we were walking in whatever woes they're facing in their present journey.

I don't think I would've learned to truly see people as image bearers if someone hadn't first seen me as if I wasn't one. I don't think I could've ever learned to love deeply and wholeheartedly without first being lied to about what love looked like. I don't believe I could've achieved expression of intimacy without an agenda unless someone first connected with me on contingency.

When we allow God to undo within us the ills that others attempted to instill, we experience healing unparalleled.

It took quite some time, but I now accept and appreciate the fact that my experience extends an opportunity to create healing in the life of someone else from the original place where I was hurt.

Where I was denied, no one else will be.

Where I was hurt, there is an opportunity for others to be healed.

Where my scars exist, I'm reminded of the sacred nature of someone else's story.

And I embrace the beauty that my belief should empower me to invite others into the fervor of my faith without the proselytization of their personhood.

This is the part where you insert your story.

Maybe you, too, were hurt by the church.

Or maybe it's a familial bond that was broken by a parent or sibling.

Maybe it's the marriage you committed to that has become flawed or failed you deeply.

The allegiance you've pledged to a country that has let you down countless times.

The list could go on into infinity.

No matter the scenario, however, it benefits no one (and you, the least) when you look forward to pain and anguish befalling the few who placed their futility on you.

This turn-the-other-cheek mentality is exceptionally difficult to embrace, but the world looks different when you infuse peace into places where the pain originated—sharing the secrets of your worth into the words you express to the world.

Breathe deep and say, "Shalom."

English (neologism), SAHN-der

# 24 Sonder

A sudden softening of the gaze. *Sonder* is the quiet epiphany that every passerby—every stranger on the street, in a car, in a window—is living a life as intricate and aching as your own.[1]

*Sonder* slowly becomes the felt awareness that each soul carries a world within itself: full of dreams, doubts, routines, and rituals you will never witness. This word gives language to an ancient truth: that no life is small, and no story is without weight.

To experience *sonder* is to be humbled into compassion—to see not just with your eyes but with your heart.

*Suffering shapes*

*the story*

*that we share*

*with the world.*

We serve a God who specializes in serving and standing with those who are suffering.

The Psalms tell us that God is near to the brokenhearted (34:18).

Both Hebrews and Deuteronomy (among others) reveal to us and remind us that God will never leave nor forsake us. The book of Ephesians (one of my personal favorites) proclaims that we serve a God who transcends all thought, exceeds imagination, and abundantly offers more than we could ever ask for.

And while all these things are true (and we will see seasons of abundance and unimaginable overflow), many of us experience stress and struggle from season to season, waiting on God to grant us His grace in the form of freedom.

As we long for the gifts of His grace, it is important to cultivate intimacy and admiration with the Giver of those gifts too.

Charles Spurgeon had this to say about scarcity:

> When the barn is full, man can live without God: when the purse is bursting with gold, we try to do without so much prayer. But once, take our gourds away, and we want our God; once cleanse the idols out of the house, then we are compelled to honor Jehovah.[2]

Scarcity is a byproduct of circumstance.

We find ourselves swept up in a situation that slows our progress or creates a sense of suffering (on a small or large scale), and the natural inclination is to attempt to undo (or avoid) whatever we're experiencing in order to restore a sense of security within ourselves.

An influx of anxious thoughts about the circumstance influences anxious emotions about the circumstance, ultimately ushering us into anxious actions. In desperation, we will do anything we can to take away the turbulence.

But scarcity (albeit natural) creates a barrier to belief.

When the resources run dry.

When money is mismanaged or mysteriously goes missing.

When the job market is at a standstill and you can't get an interview with anyone.

When the words you're whispering in prayer seem to be answered with silence.

Scarcity rears its head when expected outcomes go unanswered or go awry.

But the beauty of unanswered prayers—or the presentation of pain—exists in the invitation we're given by life to discover more of ourselves through how we respond to our situations.

No one likes to hear *no*, but I genuinely believe that it's one of the best things that can happen to us. The more obsessed we become with hearing *yes*, the less prone we'll be to respond positively to the *noes* that are guaranteed to come our way.

When I published my first book, I was an unknown, independent author with a very small platform, a few fiery ideas, and an insatiable desire to *do* just as much as I could dream. I wrote the book, produced and created all the artwork, handled most of the copyediting, drafted the concept for the cover art, and even started my own publishing house to print and produce the book myself.

The week before the pandemic began, I announced the upcoming release, and the response was unbelievable. In my one-bedroom basement apartment, I began sharing the story of the book's beginnings, fulfilling a wonderful one hundred preorders, and silently established that this would be the way forward. And for these efforts I was rewarded handsomely in a short period of time.

In just three months, I sold five hundred copies of the first run of books. The online engagement garnered thousands of followers and what felt like a small family fighting to bring the book to the forefront for the good of humanity.

A few weeks later, I got a call from Jay and Katherine Wolf requesting I come teach for a week at Hope Heals Camp, and on top of my teaching, they requested three hundred copies of the book. A week later, I got a call from a beloved university back home in West Virginia. They wanted me to come and share my story and lead their university chapel for the week, rooted in concepts that they'd read in the book too—buying nearly two hundred more copies.

These few big feats had primed my mind for *yes* in the years to come.

Just two years later, I ran into tumult. The money dried up. The speaking engagements stopped coming in as frequently. The work I'd done previously was put on pause. The job I was working had lost its wonder, and I didn't enjoy the people I was working with. I'd accrued a decent amount of debt. It went from success to what sincerely felt like suffering.

My mind couldn't comprehend *no* after experiencing an absurd amount of *yes*.

But thank God for my community—a community that championed me while winning and also lamented with me while I was losing. A close friend came to me and shared his thoughts: "You must share in the suffering before you can celebrate the success. Both require equal acceptance and attention."

That conversation changed everything for me. Call me crazy, but I genuinely believe that hearing *no* should become normal for us. When we hear *yes* too often, it can stunt our growth. The more obsessed we become with hearing *yes*, the less equipped we are to respond well when we inevitably hear *no*.

In fact, I'll take it a step further: Sometimes, *yes* is the worst thing that can happen to us.

I say this as someone who has lived through a season of perpetual *no*. And I'm grateful for it.

I've discovered more about who I am because of the *noes* I've received than I ever did from the *yeses* that I got used to. There is something sacred about scarcity—it strips away the excess and reveals the essence.

It shows us whether we truly trust God to write an unbelievable outcome in the midst of our adversity.

No matter how privileged you are or how prominent you become, people are inevitably going to tell you *no*. While *yes* is sometimes for the best, know that the *noes* are essential.

The size of the suffering that comes from the *no* will ultimately shape your story, how you understand it, and how you decide to share it.

And this is the hidden beauty of *sonder*—the reminder that while our suffering can feel deeply personal, it's never entirely private. Everyone you pass—every stranger, every friend, every person scrolling past your story—is carrying their own unseen ache, their own unanswered prayers, their own chapters of scarcity and silence.

We forget that sometimes.

We get so lost in our own longing that we miss the fact that the person next to us is fighting for hope too.

*Sonder* invites us to wonder again—not just about the roads we are walking, but about the roads others are walking beside us. It reminds us that the courage to endure the *no* might just become the exact story someone else needs to hear in their waiting.

Shalom.

French, kler-VOY-ant

# 25 Clairvoyant

From the French *clair* (clear) and *voyant* (seeing), the adjective *clairvoyant* means "clear-sighted."

Traditionally tied to mystical foresight or extrasensory perception, *clairvoyant* also speaks to the rare and sacred ability to see beyond the surface—to perceive what is not yet visible. It is a depth of insight that transcends time and circumstance, allowing one to recognize truth, possibility, and design before they've fully manifested.

To be *clairvoyant* is to witness someone's becoming before the evidence arrives. It is both gift and responsibility.

*We have to develop*

*sight that sees*

*beyond the season.*

Who we attach ourselves to is integral to the extracting—or eroding—of what exists within us, and how that inner substance eventually manifests itself in the world.

The Western world has turned me into somewhat of a cultural critic; what our society has created is a transactional tolerance that mistakes people for products. This, I believe, is encouraged by our economy of consumerism.

This unfolds in relationships, in the workplace, in spiritual spaces. People are only valued when they produce and optimize their potential. They're discarded when they lean into the pause.

But if we only ever see people *where* they are—in what they are doing—we rob them of the vision of who they *could become.*

That kind of sight requires a deeper clarity—one not bound by the season someone's currently in.

This is what it means to be truly human: to nurture a vision that uplifts others beyond their current capacity, to see past dysfunction into design, to love someone in a way that makes their future feel possible.

But this sight I'm referring to—it must also turn inward.

How we steward the holy responsibility of seeing others is directly influenced by how we first steward the responsibility of seeing ourselves.

I've been thinking lately about what we call *normal.*

About how so many of us have grown so familiar with dysfunction that peace feels foreign.

We pray for healing, but when it comes, we side-eye it.

We receive love, then brace for the loss of it.

We succeed, and immediately look for the sabotage waiting on the other side.

When life turns warm, we turn it back down.

When joy becomes sustainable, we get suspicious.

When we finally start becoming, we mourn the versions of ourselves we were supposed to outgrow. We fall into sadness when the faint echoes of the past begin to pry into our peace.

Why?

Because clarity is terrifying when all you've known is chaos.

Because being seen feels dangerous when you've spent years surviving invisibility.

Because it takes courage to stay in the room when goodness walks in.

But maybe this is what *clairvoyance* is really about—not seeing the future like a fortune teller but staying present when the future you hoped for finally starts showing up.

Maybe vision isn't about what you predict.

Maybe it's about what you're willing to receive.

Vulnerably, the last few seasons of my life have come with stress that I did not see coming.

I walked into seasons looking over my shoulder, waiting for the other shoe to drop, even when in my heart of hearts, I knew it wouldn't.

I accepted anxiety as the answer to my prayers instead of seeing the blessings that began to show up as a go-ahead from God. I let my past continue to inform my future and, in doing so, I accepted self-induced stress that I couldn't shake.

I wonder if you're someone who does the same thing—if you let old beliefs and experiences influence what you believe to be true about the future and those who exist within it.

If that's you today, here's an idea that may help.

There comes a time when we must ask if we're floating through life on someone else's raft—patched together by expectations, self-doubt, and survival skills that once saved us but cannot carry us forward.

Rafts work, but they're only meant for emergencies. And ultimately, they cannot be upheld inside life's ocean of opportunities.

If this is you, eventually you will need to accept and embrace what it means to be bold enough to build something stronger. Something honest. Something sacred enough to carry the weight of who you are truly becoming.

And when you do, you will notice a shift from feeling unsafe into stability. A stability that dares you to draw a definitive line in the sand. One that gives you the capacity and clarity enough to no longer pray prayers of familiarity that you once prayed. One that will allow you to accept that maybe, just maybe, abundance has always been after you.

Maybe it was never about seeing more.

Maybe it was always about learning to trust what is yet to be seen.

This is our hand in humanity—developing a sight that sees beyond the season, allowing individuals (and ultimately ourselves) to be uplifted despite our shortsighted circumstances.

Shalom.

(قهر), Arabic, khar

# 26 Qahr

There is no single English equivalent for the Arabic word *qahr*. It carries the weight of anger, suffering, and grief—but it is more than a passing emotion.

*Qahr* is a condition, a state of being forged through generations of unresolved oppression. It's not a flash of rage or a fleeting frustration; it's a slow simmer that takes root deep in the body and soul.

In classical Arabic literature, *qahr* was often contrasted with *lutf* (gentleness), forming a kind of divine dialectic between harshness and mercy. Over time, *qahr* came to express not just personal grief but the kind of soul-deep anguish born from systemic erasure, political repression, and cultural dislocation.

*Qahr* begins when justice is denied, when human dignity is stripped away, when voices are silenced. Imagine anger placed on a low flame, mixed with grief, persecution, and the relentless grind of systemic injustice. Over time, it becomes cellular—settling into the very DNA of those who endure it. It shapes identities and relationships.

*Beneath every brazen outburst exists a world of unheard whispers.*

Several years ago, I found myself inside a synagogue on Rosh Hashanah—celebrating the Jewish New Year alongside a body of beautiful people. This was a new space for me, a new experience, and an unforeseen exposure to Jewish roots and tradition.

I remember feeling both at ease and also eager to partake in such a sacred ceremony.

Oddly, I did not feel out of place. I sat patiently (and playfully) in my pew, Torah open, observing the environment, awaiting the arrival of the rabbi.

Service began with an undeniable beauty of rituals unfolding before me: the shofar's haunting cry, the rhythmic chants, the collective prayers, the singing of song.

Every moment was intentional and rich with meaning. It was clear that each element involved and every word spoken carried generations of memory and longing.

As the rabbi stood to deliver the sermon, he spoke about renewal. He reminded the congregation that Rosh Hashanah is not just about celebrating a new year—it's about *returning.*

Returning to the purest form of ourselves, to our callings, to our communities, and to God.

He spoke of *teshuvah* (repentance) as a way of coming back to what matters most.

He spoke about slowing down and seeing people. He spoke of apologizing upon offense.

He spoke of becoming a person of introspection and questioning amid a culture calling you to quickness and the service of self. Toward the end of his sermon, he shared an age-old story that will reverberate within the halls of my heart forever.

The tale of two monks and the woman at the river.

A senior monk and a junior monk were traveling together. At one point, they came to a river with a strong current. As the monks were preparing to cross the river, they saw a very young and beautiful woman also attempting to cross. The young woman asked if they could help her cross to the other side.

The two monks glanced at one another because they had both taken vows not to touch a woman.

Then, without a word, the older monk picked up the woman, carried her across the river, placed her gently on the other side, and carried on with his journey.

The younger monk couldn't believe what had just happened. After rejoining his companion, he was speechless, and an hour passed without a word between them.

Two more hours passed, then three. Finally, the younger monk could not contain himself any longer, and blurted out "As monks, we are not permitted [to touch] a woman, how could you then carry that woman on your shoulders?"

The older monk looked at him and replied, "Brother, hours ago I set her down on the other side of the river, why are you still carrying her?"[1]

I sat there listening, realizing that this was no different from what I had heard in all my years of visiting and gleaning from Christian churches. The messengers may have looked different, but the message was still the same through and through.

We are to meet people where they are and give them the love of God—regardless of how they look, where they're from, how they act, or what they've done. Far too often, we put parameters on who we should and shouldn't pursue and why, and our agendas keep us from connecting with those who need to know that God cares about them.

And yet, it felt new in this context. There was something profoundly human about the rabbi's call to examine our lives and repair what's broken.

On the ride home, I reflected on the message and arrived at this idea: Our perspective and practices put forth in life are influenced by our privilege and our programming.

Most of us desire to go in the same direction, but our need for navigation may look different.

Most of us articulate the area we wish to arrive at, but the language that we use differs slightly.

We let our preferences pick and choose what and who we pay attention to, what we hold in our hearts, and how we express it.

Some of us have stayed in our selfish shells of certainty for so long that we've lost the capacity to be curious about cultures we don't come from.

We tend to turn our noses up at ideas that are opposed to what we innately believe. We're quick to joust judgment at an individual before we wonder why they are the way that they've become. Why they believe what they believe.

I wonder sometimes why we aren't so inclined to adjust to or adhere to the needs of our neighbors . . . and I wonder just how helpful a singular listening ear could be to those who are whispering to the world but don't feel worthy of being heard.

We let our lenses limit us from living life alongside the people who give it purpose.

I wonder how many whispers the world is willing to share until the silence turns into a scream.

Today's poem expresses how:

***Beneath every brazen outburst exists a world of unheard whispers.***

And I would assume that all of us have arrived at an outburst—a *justified* outburst, at that. A combustion of character that simply could not be contained.

This could've sprung forth from an uncontrolled trigger, an oppressive person or people group, a trauma, or the pressure of a particular place. Wherever you choose to accuse, I'd argue that there was probably a series of silent cries that led up to said explosion . . . and if maybe someone would've listened and loved with more intention, that outburst (and all that ensued afterward) could've been avoided.

My hope is that you find both spaces of healing and people who listen . . . and that you'll reciprocate these things in relationship too.

Shalom.

Swedish, RACE-fay-ber

# 27 Resfeber

"The restless race of the traveler's heart before the journey begins, when anxiety and anticipation are tangled together."[1]

*Resfeber* is the electric pulse before movement—the quickening of breath when standing on the edge of something unknown.

It is the moment where two forces wrestle within: the excitement of possibility and the fear of what it might require. It is a feeling every traveler knows intimately, but it extends far beyond physical journeys.

*Was it an interruption . . .*

*or an invitation?*

My childhood was filled with exposure to things that fell outside of the ordinary. Many of my teenage friends were coal miners, truck drivers, or trade technicians. Not many people went to college where I come from—and, concerning conversation, the lives I lived next to made for interesting observations and ideas almost *all* the time.

We were children living very adult-oriented lives.

Many of us had jobs that we started when we were barely twelve years old. These jobs were in addition to full-time school (rarely missing a day), and we were almost always on sports teams too. With the full twenty-four hours a day, each of us made great use of nearly eighteen to twenty of them—still trying to make time to socialize and evolve into our identity.

There is a burden and a blessing in the way our lives were built, but when so much responsibility is administered so early, it equates to something like handing a child the keys to a sports car when all they know is how to accelerate (without the brakes). You don't know when or how, but a crash is almost always coming in instances such as these.

I attended my first AA meeting when I was sixteen years old. I wasn't going for myself; I was accompanying a friend of mine who had graduated high school a few years before I did.

It's springtime; I'm cozy in my room on a summer afternoon. Xbox controller in hand, headset on conversing with my friends, and then I faintly hear my mother shout my name from the living room . . . and something in her tone is out of the ordinary. I put the headset down and head to the living room to find my friend. He's standing in the doorway, and he doesn't look too well.

His nose is runny, his eyes are red, and he's vulnerably asking me in front of my mother if I will attend a meeting with him. I look at my mother; she gives me eyes that empower me to make whatever decision I deem right.

I don't even think twice. I go back to my room and turn off my game console, I grab the closest pair of shoes, I head back to the living room to meet my friend, and we go to his meeting.

I sat through the whole thing too—introduced myself and was honest about why I came. I even saw other people I knew there. It was a formative experience that a typical teenager shouldn't have, but its imprint still lives on in my brain.

Was it an interruption . . . or an invitation?

Sixteen years later, I'm still holding the weight of that question and often examining my experiences and expectations of others.

In that AA meeting, someone submitted a psychological saying: *You spot it, you got it.*

It's an expression that shines a light on our shortsightedness, exposing how we often assume—casting judgment when we see something in someone else instead of stepping back to first look at ourselves.

"You spot it, you got it" is more than a catchy phrase—it's a mirror we often refuse to look into. It speaks to the way we see traits in others, whether admirable or aggravating, and fail to recognize that we're really just encountering fragments of ourselves. When something irritates us in another person, it's often because it touches a nerve in our own story.

Maybe we've spent years shedding a version of ourselves that we now see reflected back in someone else, and instead of extending grace, we recoil. Or maybe it's a part of ourselves we haven't yet confronted—a blind spot hiding in plain sight. Either way, *projection* is a quiet, insidious thing.

It allows us to point outward when we should be looking inward.

It permits us to critique from a distance rather than get close enough to understand anyone, because it's easier to condemn than to consider.

But what if, instead of reacting, we paused? What if every time we spotted something we were quick to judge, we asked, *Why does this bother me? What part of me does this reflect?* Because if we were willing to sit with the discomfort, we might realize that we are not as separate from the people we critique as we think we are.

Today's word, *resfeber*, invites us to hold a heavy weight—one that can be the prelude to progress.

Yes, this word is about traveling, but it also captures the very nature of *transformation*. Giving a nod to that split second between staying and going, between holding on and letting go.

It is the space where hesitation meets courage, and where uncertainty becomes the precursor to discovery. *Resfeber* is more than just a moment in time; it is a mirror of the human experience.

What if our hesitation before change is not just nervous energy but a *sacred threshold*—one that asks us to decide, over and over again, whether we will lean into the unknown or retreat into the familiar?

It is easier to project than to process.

Easier to dismiss than to dig deeper.

Easier to critique than to contemplate.

Easier to cast off than to come close.

But we can build the capacity for a new condition . . . one that allows us to embody empathy over irritation.

In every interaction exists an opportunity to *actually* see someone.

Beyond their presentation, beyond their language or their lifestyle.

If we stop for just a second and choose not to judge but to join, life will lend us more lessons than we knew we needed.

If we don't stop to wonder how they got there.

If we don't consider the experiences that shaped them.

If we don't acknowledge that everyone grows the way they have been treated.

If we don't stop to ask, "Is this an interruption . . . or an invitation?"

We miss the boat on beauty.

Maybe the real weight of *resfeber* is that it asks us to be brave enough to sit in the tension—to feel the discomfort of confrontation without rushing toward dismissal.

To let the mirror reflect what it must, without shattering it in self-defense.

If we only ever see interruptions, we will miss the invitations tucked inside them—the chance to understand, to stretch, to soften. The choice is ours, and it is not a one-time decision but a daily discipline: Will we react, or will we reflect? Will we remain tethered to our projections, or will we loosen our grip on the assumptions that keep us from real connection?

If we are willing to see beyond the surface, we might just realize that every irritation holds insight, every friction carries formation, and every moment of hesitation is really just a doorway, waiting for us to walk through.

Shalom.

English, si-ko-FAN-tik

# 28 Sycophantic

To be *sycophantic* is to adopt a demeanor of excessive flattery or submissiveness, often at the expense of integrity or authenticity.

It reflects a transactional approach to relationships, where actions are guided by self-serving motives rather than genuine care or respect. A sycophantic individual operates in a dynamic of asymmetry—seeking favor or proximity to power through manipulation or insincerity.

The word calls attention to how flattery and manipulation can distort relationships and erode trust.

*Life lives*

*at the end*

*of the leap.*

What does it mean to live truthfully in a world where validation often carries a price? The word *sycophantic* challenges us to pause and examine our motivations.

In today's reality of relationships, it's important to stop often and ask: Am I moving from love, from a place of genuine care and concern, or am I performing to win favor?

Across history and cultures, sycophancy has been a tool used for survival in hierarchical structures, from ancient courts to corporate offices. Politicians lobbying for more power have colluded behind the scenes to get bills blocked or passed based on their love (or lack thereof) for their contemporaries. Roman citizens used to barter and trade, backdooring deals or fixing the outcome of events to be relieved of their debts or gain favor among their superiors. In many ways, by and large, sycophancy critiques the imbalance of power and highlights the moral compromises made in the pursuit of advantage.

The concept is a mirror to human fragility—an exploration of the fear of rejection, the need for validation, and the social power dynamics that compel individuals to sacrifice their authenticity.

To live sycophantically is to compromise one's own agency, reducing human connection to mere utility. It raises a question of value: *What do we lose when we trade truth for approval?*

But approval is only necessary when one has been accused . . . when one is looking for evidence to inform ideas against their own inherent identity. Oddly enough, the etymology of the word *sycophancy* gives a nod to its Greek roots—often translating into "informer" or "accuser."

A literal expression of unjustified prosecution of your person.

Personally, I've come to recognize my accuser as my inner critic, often arising during times of individual ascension.

It's the tension that tightens your chest when a colleague compliments you.

It's the onset of self-sabotage that you allow after fighting to overcome your old ways.

It's affirmation arriving at your doorstep, knocking and asking for entry, but your refusing to let it in due to doubt and delusion. It's the ping-pong you play with your personality, trying to decide what route to take each day you wake up—one of empowerment or one of accusation.

Empowerment is the choice that bargains on your behalf for belief. Accusation is the agreement with and surrender to the lie that you don't deserve what you have—or that you'll never rise from the valley you're traversing.

It's the rising right of refusal against oneself anytime you begin to earn something. It's your doubts telling you that you don't deserve it.

What we internalize in our identity informs our belief system and is ultimately the baseline for our behavior.

This is why projection is such a prominent part of our culture today, and why it has become so difficult to discern who is being real with you in relationship, and who is taking your interactions as a transaction.

Maybe you feel it from time to time in others, or maybe even in yourself—the invisible gauge that's oscillating in every interaction, slowly sliding from authenticity to self-service.

This gauge is bolstered by belief.

Whatever you believe is whatever you become.

If you don't believe that you're worthy, you will express this in how you interact with anyone.

If you believe that others are interacting with you only out of utility, always trying to achieve something, you'll stay skeptical and always assume that anyone you interact with isn't authentic.

If you don't believe you're loved or cared for, your emotions will lead you astray in many ways.

If you don't believe the life you're after is also after you, you'll continue to spiral and stay dissatisfied, spinning in circles. If you don't believe that anyone wants to love you and receive you as you are, you'll subconsciously associate distrust with anyone who wants to go deep with you.

I've learned these things through honest examination of self, spiritual revelation, and (most recently) a psychological concept called the *mirror principle.*

The mirror principle suggests that our external world reflects our internal reality.

It posits that what we perceive in others—whether admiration, judgment, or irritation—is often a projection of what resides within us.[1]

In simpler terms, the way we see the world and the people around us is shaped by what we believe about ourselves.

This truth is a weight that anchors down most of humanity. It's nothing that we want to carry, but because of what has happened to us, the way we've been hurt, and how we've yet to heal, we continue to deal in our insecurities and ultimately allow them to influence our interactions with everyday individuals.

So how do we overcome?

We embrace the fact that life lives at the end of the leap.

We accept that vulnerability is a prerequisite to removing the power from our flawed perception of our internal world and the external worlds all around us. We allow ourselves to deal with the discomfort that comes from arriving with authenticity, even when others are maliciously motivated.

Sycophancy is hell on a hamster wheel . . . and with this one little life that you get, there is a beautiful rebellion found in abandoning the behavior that refuses to allow you access to the most authentic parts of your identity that the world is in desperate need of.

And maybe that's the final caution and the quiet calling of *sycophancy*—that if we're not careful, we'll spend so much time curating how we're perceived that we'll forget how to *actually connect*.

Because real connection requires truth.

And real relationships require trust. The danger isn't just that we might perform for approval—it's that we might become so fluent in performance that we no longer recognize sincerity in ourselves or in others.

So guard your heart, but keep it soft. Move in love, but keep it honest. And wherever you go, lead with what is real—because that's the only thing capable of meeting another human soul where it actually lives.

Shalom.

(ἀμετάθετος), Greek, ah-meh-TAH-theh-tos

# 29 Ametathetos

*Ametathetos* is a word used to describe that which cannot change—not out of stubbornness, but out of holy design. Often used to speak of the nature of God, it's more than just permanence; it is an essence sealed in certainty. In a world where everything moves, morphs, and fades, *ametathetos* names the One who stays—standing alone in sheer reverence.

It is the still point in the storm. The foundation beneath the feeling. The reminder that faith is not rooted in predictability but in presence—the kind that doesn't flinch when we do. To call something *ametathetos* is to say, "This can be trusted. This will not leave."

*Every "I don't know"*

*that you have uttered*

*has always been*

*enough for God.*

We often don't engage with God because of what we *don't* know, not because of what we *do* know. If communion is an ongoing conversation that we are invited into rather than a performance we must perfect, would we not be more inclined to step toward Him instead of pulling away? But in our unknown, we throw feelings into the void—diluting the facts of God and giving more room to worry than to His will.

Trust and transparency are undeniable fruits of any relationship that has been tested and tried. We learn this in our earthly interactions, but the wisdom we witness can be easily transferred into our eternal one—if we let it.

I love how, in Matthew 6, Jesus taught His disciples not to be like the hypocrites who prayed in the synagogues and in the streets, boasting poetic prayers, letting their words work for them to impress the eyes and ears of observing individuals.

Instead, He said to pray in secret, not as a performance but as communion—where intention and honesty shape the connection.

Communion does not demand certainty. It only requires presence.

We imagine that God's love must have conditions because human love often does. That if we have wandered, we must first fix ourselves before returning. That if we have fallen short, God's patience must have too.

But this is not who He is.

A time too many, we place a perspective on God shaped by our experience with earthly individuals. Doubt, delusion, disappointment, discontentment. Being lied to, looked down upon, leaned on and into for all the wrong things.

By your parents, by your siblings, by romantic partners, coworkers, or spiritual authority. All of us are people who have been perpetually paralyzed by the activities and intentions of another.

And the emotional toll is all too exhausting, leading us into spirals that affect our spiritual lives.

In an era where many have access to excess, it has become exceptionally difficult for much of humanity to follow the urge to partake in the divine.

We consume, we distract, we numb.

We don't calculate the cost of communion because we have been conditioned to see stimulation as an acceptable substitute for solitude. We reach for what is quick and comforting, instead of leveraging the long road that makes us come face-to-face with our frustrations—believing God's in stride with us as we step.

I have done this. Perhaps you have too.

Personally, this reality has been the root cause of my wrestling with image, identity, and communion overall.

Misinformation, frustration, and a lack of proximity to God often left me with questions I did not know how to answer.

Ones that weighed on my heart and mind, keeping me bound by my disbelief.

I've learned about beauty not through belonging but through exclusion—through the warped ideas and misunderstandings that others projected onto me. But as I sit in solitude, I see the world through my spiritual set of eyes—learning to recognize what's misaligned and course-correct through communion.

God's presence is not subject to our inconsistencies. He does not disappear when we falter. He does not withdraw when we doubt. He is immutable. His nature does not shift because ours does. And communion with Him is not a reward for perfection—it is the means by which we are made whole. It's the setting by which shalom is shaped inside us.

So if communion is not about performance but presence, if God is not waiting for us to perfect our approach but simply to show up—then why do we hesitate? Why do we allow uncertainty to build a wall between us and the One who has never wavered? Perhaps it is not knowledge we lack but trust.

Many of us today are a breath away from a breakthrough, but our failure to make fancy words or pray the perfect prayer is the very thing standing between us and the spiritual solutions to our ongoing issues.

I've learned that spiritual maturity is developed and measured by how much unhelpful information you're willing to leave behind and unlearn, so that your soul can be reshaped by what is true.

It can be ugly, it can be beautiful, it can be broken, or it can be bare. It doesn't have to sound poetic or feel powerful.

You don't have to have all the words or know how to do it perfectly.

I will genuinely argue that:

***Every "I don't know" you've ever spoken has always been enough for God.***

And maybe today, your honesty and "I don't know" are the catalysts that show you just how much God cares.

I'm curious: What keeps you from being honest with God?

What narrative have you accepted about what qualifies you for closeness?

And where did that narrative come from—God, or your experience with people?

Because if God is truly *ametathetos*—unchanging, unwavering, constant—then He doesn't flinch when we bring Him our confusion. He doesn't withdraw when we come undone. If He is communal by nature, then showing up in all your uncertainty is not only allowed—it may be the most sacred thing you'll ever do.

And maybe the gift of that communion is not only healing for you but also a gracious gift for all those you're connected to.

Shalom.

( الصمت ), Arabic, ALL-samt

# 30 Al-Samt

This Arabic expression is translated into "silence," meaning to refrain from speaking falsehood rather than truth.

In English, while "silence" captures part of its essence, the depth of *al-samt* often depends on context, particularly its spiritual and philosophical implications.

In Arabic, it's a rich concept tied not only to the absence of sound but also to the presence of wisdom and reverence. In many Arabic-speaking cultures, silence is often associated with wisdom, introspection, and a deeper connection to the divine.[1] Silence is seen as a way to listen to one's inner voice or the voice of God. Sometimes, silence is more powerful than words in resolving conflicts or expressing emotions.

The concept is deeply embedded in Arabic poetry and literature, symbolizing unspoken truths, emotional depth, or moments of profound realization.

*The man who speaks because*

*he can is such a tyrant . . .*

*neglecting strength in words*

*that must emerge from silence.*

I met a man named Dave Gibbons in Nashville, Tennessee.

Dave was one of the final speakers at a conference that I was attending, and in his thirty minutes or so onstage, he laid out some compelling, challenging ideas and wildly prophetic perspectives.

After his time of teaching, I approached him to the side of the stage to pick his brain. I had a flight to catch, and there was a line of people piling up behind me, trying to get access to his ideas and encouragement too. We instantly connected, but he could tell that I was in somewhat of a hurry, so he was kind enough to offer me his number and told me to give him a call next week.

So I did.

Toward the end of our nearly hour-long call, he gave me some homework. He said:

> Nigel, I want you to sit down sometime this week or next and draw a straight line on a piece of paper. This line represents the timeline of your life. Cut off the end and envision it from age zero, all the way up to the age you are today. Then, sit with the Holy Spirit and ask God to reveal your highest moments and lowest moments in life—the traumas, the heartbreaks, the mountaintop experiences. When you're done, think long and hard about the connection between everything above the line and below it . . . and I promise, if you're patient enough, your purpose in life will reveal itself through the significance of your experience.[2]

The idea of intentionally revisiting some of the most difficult and scarring moments from my past, matched with acknowledging and enjoying the most beautiful experiences too, was heavy homework.

I thought about that exercise nearly every day for a year, and although I've admittedly never physically followed through with it, I have sat in silence, making a mental map out of each of those moments, stringing together what I believe to be their significance.

I've learned that it's not until you slow down that you can see the things that are seeking your emotions and attention. Each of us, in our individuality, are the makeup of many moments passed. We've been slowly and silently shaped and molded by these moments, our experiences, and the ideas we've given time and attention to that ultimately form the byproduct of our belief.

Dubb Alexander once said: "Your place of pain will become your place of reign."[3] He was implying that pressing into the issues that have ailed you actually removes the power that any of these issues have over you. This happens through your perspective and imagination being reshaped as you address the moments that "made" you.

Personally, I've watched my perspective transform my life as I've revisited ailments and issues from my past. In the deep work that I've done with my therapist, we often arrive at the question: Can we acknowledge that God was there while the damage was being done?

And after I ask this question, and apply honesty to it, it not only tests and refines my faith; it renews my mind in the present moment. Had these hardships not occurred, I wouldn't have the story that I do. Had this issue not needed to be overcome, I'd have far less resilience.

These are my sentiments for my story. I wonder what words could arise from yours?

As you do this work, it's as if you're walking a long hallway of echoes that you silenced in previous seasons . . . and as you near the end of it, you see that your soul has been speaking to you, asking your heart for the attention that it has so desperately needed to heal.

Many of us have been spiritually and emotionally conditioned to believe that silence equates to absence, but I believe that silence is actually a sacred space where truth reveals itself.

Distractions lead us into disbelief, however. Having access to excess every day has demented and disabled our ability to sit in silence and deal with the discomfort that comes from days doused in confusion and call us to patience.

Silence is like the crucible, a furnace that forcefully burns away our "need" for the unnecessary, longing to leave only that which is essential and sacred. And the crucible shares similarities with the sanctuary, requiring silence as a prerequisite to find refuge and clarity.

Both spaces are perfectly primed for you to meet God and experience Him in the fullness of His character.

God, in His infinite complexity, reveals Himself as both sanctuary and crucible. He is love, compassion, and gentleness—but He is also holiness, justice, and refinement. In the same way a parent teaches their child obedience by withholding instant gratification, God teaches us through moments of silence and waiting. He doesn't always give us what we want when we want it, because true growth requires discipline, not indulgence.

Scripture shows us this tension beautifully.

The book of James reminds us that when we take a single step toward God, He also takes steps toward us (4:8). Yet the closer we get, the more we see Him as He truly is—sometimes vastly different from what we expected or wanted. He is not only the Gift Giver but the Gift itself, and when we enter His presence, we begin to see ourselves more clearly.

Like a great mirror, God shows us every part of who we are—the sacred and the broken—and invites us to surrender it all to Him.

This is why the sanctuary, the place of safety, can sometimes feel like a crucible.

It will not tolerate anything unholy. The heart cries out for healing and holiness, and in God's presence, everything else is stripped away. This is the reason why priests in ancient times had ropes tied around their waists when entering the holy of holies. If they were not clean, they would fall, and others would have to pull them out.

God's holiness is not just a concept; it is a reality that transforms and refines.

In our lives, we encounter people who feel like sanctuaries—individuals whose presence both comforts and challenges us. They are crucibles, showing us what is possible when we surrender to God, and they reflect His love and holiness in a way that calls us higher.

These encounters remind us that silence is not emptiness. It is the space where God speaks most clearly, where He burns away what doesn't belong and reveals what is true.

Silence, then, is not the absence of sound but the presence of God.

It is golden because it makes space for wisdom, healing, and transformation. May we learn to embrace the silence, to sit in the sanctuary and endure the crucible, knowing that both spaces are sacred and necessary for our growth.

Today, this has become exceptionally difficult for many of us due to our desire to have things our way, always. Due to our inability to take an honest rebuke from a brother or sister, valuing the perspective of our reputation over the reality of our actions.

I love the sentiment my mother always used to share: God gave you two ears and one mouth so that you can listen so much more than you speak.

Some of us have never been silenced.

Some of us have never had our freedom forced away from us.

Some of us have an undeveloped discipline of listening first.

Some of us are reactors, not responders.

And the sum of us affects some of us.

Until we learn what it means to let silence inform how we share, we'll be walking squawk boxes—wasting words, expressing emptiness, and expecting others to show up and sit beneath the sound of our voice when we really have nothing to say.

As easy as it is to remain unchanged and unchallenged, I pray you live a bit more loosely, letting those around you lift you up in love and speak into what they see—shaping the way you share.

Shalom.

(ποίημα), Greek, poy-EH-ma

# 31 Poiēma

A crafted work—not merely made, but made with meaning. *Poiēma* is the word from which we get *poem*, but in its ancient roots it carried broader weight: a masterpiece, a work shaped by intention, design, and care. In Scripture, it is used to describe humanity itself—we are God's *poiēma*, not accidents, but artistry (Ephesians 2:10).

To be a *poiēma* is to be evidence of a Maker's imagination, an embodied idea made visible through flesh and spirit. It is the claim that creation is not random but revelatory, and that every life carries the fingerprint of its Author.

*To many, being seen and known is a fight;*

*to others, being seen and known is a right.*

*The page ain't turning,*
*yet the heart's still yearning,*
*and the soul is still,*
*stitching in its bed.*
*The chapter stays instead.*
*Another book upon a dusty shelf,*
*somehow remains unread.*
*Strung out sentences on every page . . .*
*Some loose-leaf lit with love, others filled*
*with fits of rage.*
*Purpose piled within each word:*
*every adjective, noun, and verb.*
*Doing jumping jacks on every page,*
*just begging to be heard.*
*But this book was written backwards . . .*
*and contingent on its factors*
*it has the choice to choose*
*to fall within one's hands.*
*So even if the heart starts beating,*
*and someone finds this book worth reading . . .*
*It'd take a special kind of soul to*
*understand.*

"Liberty Island" by Nigel Darius, 2025

Poetry and art have always carried a mystic quality, a connection to something supernatural that transcends earthly understanding.

In many ancient cultures poets and prophets were intertwined, their roles often indistinguishable. The Ancient Near East, for example, revered those who spoke in poetic form, believing their words carried a divine resonance. To speak beautifully—to weave language into something transcendent—was to access a realm that felt sacred, as if heaven itself had granted them the ability to articulate truths that an ordinary vocabulary could not.

Philosophically, poetry and art transcend time because they engage both the heart and the mind. They offer not just explanations but invitations—calling us to feel, reflect, and imagine.

Art is not confined to logic; it stretches beyond reason, often evoking emotions and insights that words alone cannot contain. Poetry is not just a medium of beauty; it is a language of healing, giving voice to pain, joy, and the unspoken complexities of being human.

It teaches us that beauty, even when born of brokenness, can be redemptive.

James Baldwin once said: "You think your pain and your heartbreak are unprecedented in the history of the world, but then you read. It was Dostoevsky and Dickens that taught me that the things that tormented me most were the very things that connected me with all the people who were alive, or who had ever been alive."[1]

This is what poetry has always been for me—a gracious glimpse inside the soul of a person, artfully expressed ideas and experiences. Subtle ways to warm you, letting you know you're not alone.

I learned about the word *poiēma* while reading the book of Ephesians. In chapter 2, verse 10, we get a clear picture of the apostle

Paul declaring: "For we are God's handiwork [*poiēma*], created in Christ Jesus to do good works, which God prepared in advance for us to do."

This suggests that *every* human life is a *divine masterpiece*, intricately designed to embody God's creativity and purpose.

If the pages are prewritten and prescribed by God Himself, our obligation as His creation is to discover how to learn and live our lines (in a way that properly unpacks the poem).

Society and culture do a wonderful job at attempting to not only add unnecessary lines to our stories, but completely rewrite the story if we let them.

In a time when culture attempts to curate your inner world, in a society that is always attempting to tell you who you are, and in an era when churches are always trying to change you instead of challenge you, we are tasked with protecting our poems and understanding what and who sits at the intersection of our story.

The Bible tells us that we are one body with many parts . . . and amid times of tension, when seeking solutions, we all need to be our part of the body.

> Imagine a body. A single entity with many parts—hands, feet, eyes, ears—each with its unique role. Now, imagine if one part of the body decided it wasn't important because it wasn't like another part. What if the foot resented not being a hand or the ear felt less significant because it wasn't an eye? Would the body still function as it should? Of course not. Every part has its purpose, and together they make the body whole. (1 Corinthians 12:12–27, my paraphrase)

This is my summary of the apostle Paul's approach to explaining how we are one body with many parts, and all of us hold a separate significance. He used this metaphor to teach that every person—regardless of background, skill set, race, ethnicity, or social status—is essential in God's plan. Just as the body thrives when its parts work together, so does the community of faith, which Paul calls the body of Christ. Each person is uniquely placed by God to fulfill a specific purpose. No one is insignificant, and no one is independent of the others.

This unity isn't about uniformity. It's about celebrating diversity while working toward a shared purpose. When one part suffers, the whole body feels the pain. When one part is honored, the whole body rejoices. The heart of this passage is simple: *We are interconnected, and our collective well-being depends on valuing every individual's contribution.*

So . . . what does any of this have to do with you?

You need to know today that the One who created you has already written your story and signed off on the power of your poem; there is no further achievement or striving required to become.

This is why I say:

***To many, being seen and known is a fight,***
***to others, being seen and known is a right.***

Be comforted today in these kind words, knowing that no job title, no annual salary, no relationship status, no socioeconomic situation—or any other identifier—gets to tell you who you are or whose you are. Your becoming is a birthright. Don't be confused by our culture and compromise your identity, taking on a mantle that minimizes who we were meant to be.

Despite what we do, despite what we've done, despite where we're from—this is true of us. That we've been seen and known since our conception, and the God of heaven and earth adores us.

Shalom.

English (derived from Greek), or-thuh-PRAK-see

# 32 Orthopraxy

Right practice. *Orthopraxy* is the lived embodiment of one's belief—the mirror held to one's theology by way of their habits, ethics, and everyday choices. Where *orthodoxy* speaks to right belief, *orthopraxy* asks: Does your body carry what your mouth proclaims?

It is the fusion of faith and action, the refusal to let convictions remain disembodied. In sacred tension, it exposes the gap between what we preach and how we live. *Orthopraxy* calls us out of performative belief and into practiced love, not as a performance, but as proof.

*The dichotomy stands in our pursuit of the Savior, how we preach holy belief yet have heretical behavior.*

You can hide your hand, but you cannot hide your heart.

These words came flowing from my fingers on MLK Day this past year as I sat discontent, scrolling social media on my phone.

Every year on such a sacred day, my timeline fills with his face, his quotes, and beautifully curated posts. The imagery is stirring, and the words are familiar, but I often wonder: *How many people who share these posts truly embody the principles that Dr. King lived and died for?*

How many of us are willing to go beyond the veneer of thinly veiled solidarity and step into the messy, demanding work of justice, reconciliation, and love in action? It's easy to repost a quote. It's much harder to align our lives with the radical call embedded within those words.

Dr. Martin Luther King Jr. once said, "The church must be reminded that it is not the master or the servant of the state, but rather the conscience of the state. It must be the guide and the critic of the state, and never its tool."[1] These words carry the weight of a challenge—a challenge that, decades later, still feels unmet.

The dissonance I experience on this day mirrors a larger problem within modern Christianity, particularly in the West. The church has so deeply in this day become the state's tool—aligning itself with political power, cultural supremacy, and exclusionary practices that fracture communities rather than heal them.

The American gospel, as it has been called, is not the gospel of Jesus Christ.

It is a gospel of additions, where the cross is adorned with flags, platforms, and ideologies that distort its message. And this is the tension that we must tackle today . . . one that exists between our orthodoxy and orthopraxy.

*Orthodoxy* is the proclamation of truth: that Jesus Christ, through

His life, death, and resurrection, accomplished all that was necessary for our salvation.

As Ephesians 2:8–9 declares: "It is by grace you have been saved, through faith—and this is not from yourselves, it is the gift of God—not by works, so that no one can boast."

But *orthopraxy* is where this truth takes shape in our lives. It is how we live out what we believe. And too often, the dichotomy between what we preach and how we practice exposes a lack of alignment.

Dr. King understood this. He understood that belief without action is hollow, that orthodoxy without orthopraxy is hypocrisy. He modeled a faith that listened before it spoke, loved before it judged, and walked in proximity to the marginalized. His legacy is a reminder that the gospel is not a set of words or doctrines to be weaponized, but instead, a life lived in radical love for God and neighbor.

This is why the American gospel is so dangerous. It adds to the cross, turning it into a symbol of exclusion rather than invitation. It aligns itself with power, using God's name to justify oppression, idolatry, and injustice.

It forgets that Jesus' life was spent with the very people whom society rejected—the outcasts, the sinners, the oppressed, and those who were living wildly different earthly lives, ones that did not reflect the heart of eternity.

The true gospel does not need additions. It does not need political parties, cultural supremacy, or performative acts of solidarity. It needs lives transformed by grace, lived in love, and marked by justice. *Orthopraxy* demands that our beliefs move from words into action and that our lives become a reflection of the Jesus we proclaim.

The cross of Christ is not a hammer of authority that one wields to isolate and exclude; it is instead a tool of invitation into humility that can heal the heart of all humanity.

Jesus demonstrated a love that was gentle and lowly. His actions, motivated by love, reinforced the theological truth that all humanity inherently bears the image of God. He was honest and carried Himself with integrity, and although He lived within an unjust Roman government, He did not conform to His environment for power. He instead gave His power away so that you and I could share in the sweet, sacred, sacrificial love of God that saves and sanctifies. He lived counterculturally, and in His infinite wisdom, He showed us what the gospel embodies.

His is a gospel that listens, learns, and lives in proximity to the pain of others.

So where do you and I fit into this story?

Our task is to take an honest look at our own lives and ask: Are we living the gospel we proclaim? Are our hands aligned with our hearts, or are we hiding behind veneers of belief that mask a lack of love?

The dichotomy stands in our pursuit of the Savior: How can we preach holy belief yet have heretical behavior?

Orthodoxy without orthopraxy is a denial of the very faith we claim to hold.

To live out the true gospel is to follow the Jesus who loved without condition, served without expectation, and sacrificed without reservation. It is to live in such a way that people walk away from our presence knowing they've encountered the heart of God, not through our words, but through our actions.

This is the essence of orthopraxy: belief made visible, love made tangible.

So here is my challenge: Lay down the idols you've added to the cross.

Stop hiding your hand while your heart remains unchanged.

Let your life reflect the radical, sacrificial love of Christ. Because in the end, the world doesn't need more empty performances or curated quotes. It needs people whose hearts are so aligned with the love of God that their hands cannot help but follow.

Shalom.

German, OOM-felt

# 33 Umfeld

The word *Umfeld* is a German term that translates loosely into English as "environment," "surroundings," or "context," but its meaning goes beyond these simple definitions. It encompasses not only the physical environment but also the social, cultural, and psychological influences that shape an individual or situation.[1]

*Umfeld* challenges us to consider how our surroundings—both seen and unseen—affect our sense of self, spiritual practice, and relationships with others. It invites reflection on the interplay between the external factors that mold us and the internal choices we make in response.

*Sometimes it isn't an*

*issue of the seeds,*

*it's an issue of the soil.*

As a child, I was endlessly curious. My mind was a playground for questions and connections, constantly soaking up my surroundings like a sweet little sponge.

I loved words—writing them, memorizing them, rapping them, making sense of their meanings. This curiosity and passion for learning flourished in many classrooms as a kid, but not every environment nurtured my growth or natural gifts.

In fact, a hallmark moment in third grade would shape my understanding of identity and individuality, and how those two things are forever affected by our environment, for years to come.

My teacher at the time didn't see my curiosity as a gift . . . and as she dealt with it daily, she deemed it a disruption. One day in particular, we began a memory exercise where twenty words were written on the width of the chalkboard. We had several minutes to sit and study them. Shortly after, they would be erased and it was our obligation to recall as many words from memory as we could with as much time as we needed afterward.

I just so happened to finish long before the other students. In my excitement, I couldn't keep quiet and began engaging with my classmates—a behavior innocent in my mind but chaotic in hers. My teacher snapped. She bolted from her chair, grabbed my arm, and yanked me out of my seat. In front of the entire class, she declared that I wasn't "normal." Worse still, she said I was mentally impaired and needed to be immediately placed in "slow classes."

Exiled to the hallway, I waited for my mother to arrive. When she did, things only escalated. My teacher told her that my disruptive behavior and supposed lack of intelligence were likely the result of her "mixing with a Black man." The more the words sank in, the more they stung.

A week after the heated exchange, she demanded that I be tested for special education.

So I was.

The results from the tests she demanded would soon reveal a very different story.

Not only was I not in need of remedial class or special education, but the results revealed that I actually belonged in the "gifted" program—an advanced curriculum designed for high-performing students who needed more engagement than the average classroom could provide.

This experience taught me a powerful truth: Sometimes, the problem isn't the seed but the soil.

My potential wasn't limited by who I was but by the environment I was placed in—one where prejudice and impatience stifled growth instead of fostering it. The soil of that classroom was toxic, incapable of nourishing the seeds of curiosity and creativity within me. Yet, when the soil was changed, my growth was garnered.

What about you?

Have you ever mistaken your own worth for the failure of your environment?

What beauty in you might be lying dormant, not because it's absent, but because the soil hasn't seen it yet?

*Umfeld* is a reminder that our progress as people is never just about the seed; it's about the environment that influences it—the soil, the care, and the unseen factors that shape us.

In this instance I'm reminded of Jesus' parable of the sower in Matthew 13, where He illustrates this idea so eloquently. Seeds scattered on rocky soil or among thorns struggle to grow, while seeds in good soil thrive and produce a bountiful harvest.

The quality of the soil determines the fruitfulness of the seed, just as the quality of our surroundings shapes our ability to flourish.

We often blame ourselves when we struggle to grow; we get upset when our outcome doesn't match the input, or our merit doesn't reap the reward, not realizing that the soil we've surrendered to may not actually be working for us but against us.

Toxic relationships, unhealthy professional environments, and societal biases can stunt our potential, no matter how strong the seed within us may be.

Conversely, when we cultivate rich soil—communities of support, spaces of encouragement, and environments of love—our growth becomes not just possible but inevitable.

This principle also calls us to examine the soil we provide for others. As humans, our role is not only to deal with the worst parts of people but also to seek and nurture the best in them. We are called to be gardeners of one another's potential, cultivating conditions where growth can take root. This requires patience, empathy, and a willingness to believe in the unseen possibilities within each person.

My third-grade teacher's words could have crushed me . . . and under circumstances of submissiveness, they probably would have. But instead, those words and unforeseen obstacles became fertilizer for my growth.

The transition to the gifted program was a reminder that the soil matters, and when we are placed in the right environment, the seeds of our potential can bloom. This truth is as personal as it is universal. Whether we are sowing into our own lives or the lives of others, the quality of the soil—the *Umfeld*—determines the harvest.

Take a moment to examine the soil around you.

What influences are shaping your growth?

What conditions are nurturing (or hindering) the seeds of potential within you?

And just as importantly, how are you cultivating the soil for those around you?

Remember, the garden doesn't flourish because of the seed alone. It thrives because of the care it receives, the nourishment it absorbs, and the space it's given to grow.

See your seeds and soil as sacred.

Shalom.

(תִּיקּוּן עוֹלָם), Hebrew, tee-KOON oh-LAHM

# 34 Tikkun Olam

To repair the world, not as a metaphor, but as a mandate.

*Tikkun olam* is the call to co-create justice, to restore what has been fractured, and to bring light to places dimmed by despair.

Rooted in Jewish tradition, it is more than charity or activism; it is sacred responsibility. It teaches that every act of healing—public or private, global or personal—is a stitch in the fabric of renewal. And so, the work begins inward: to mend what is broken in us so we may mend what is broken around us. To practice *tikkun olam* is to believe that wholeness is possible, and worth the labor.

*I'm not cursed,*

*I'm just the first.*

I have always been fascinated by apologists.

People who have the educational foundation, courage, and commitment not just to stand on a stage and evangelize an audience, but stand firm on open floors filled with questioning, curiosity, and critique.

Those who have prepared a defense for their faith—patiently waiting for people to potentially poke holes in a set of beliefs that they've committed their entire lives to.

In most arguments about ethics and morality, non-Christians argue this point: "We should all make it into heaven if we do to others what we want to be done to us. I'm not a bad person; I'm a good person—that's why I should go to heaven."

There is typically no theological backing to these points. Most arguments are often expressions fueled by emotion. And occasionally you'll have a misquoted Bible verse that is lacking context but used convincingly for the sake of the prosecutor's argument.

The textbook response from an apologist is to ask: "Well . . . who determines a basis for what is good and what is bad? Where does the motive of morality come from?"

The conversation will oscillate between ideas of collective consciousness and societal standards. Typically, the Bible is mentioned, too, alongside other ancient religious texts, but it always comes back to the question of what it means to be good.

Amid the arguments of what it means to be good, I think both the apologist and the agitated miss a very essential message. And that message in question form is:

What is the benefit to being good?

And if I begin to be "good," is there an incentive for my actions?

In recent years it's safe to say that there has been a significant dip in humanity's desire to do good. Connection to our neighbor has become co-opted by capitalism, creating a deep divide between what used to be normal among the neighborly. We've pushed one another into isolation, and the struggle of learned loneliness is pushing/influencing our ideas of individualism and independence to their apex. I learned recently that before the 1960s, neighborhoods used to operate in unity and co-dependence.[1] Instead of a twenty-member community enmeshed in a cul-de-sac buying lawnmowers separately to use at their individual homes, they would put their money together to purchase community resources, quite literally sharing the wealth among one another on a system of honor and intentionality.[2]

Today, we're not taught to embody an idea such as this. The term *codependence* has become taboo and is often looked at as a trait of the weak-hearted when, in reality, the need to depend on your neighbor used to be a primary pillar that made the world turn.

Across the past few decades, wealth has been devalued in terms of community dependence and now is determined by the amount held within your bank account.

Events like the Los Angeles wildfires in January 2025 have opened our eyes to this overwhelming issue of insulation—watching "wealthy" people call on private fire departments to come and fight the fires and protect their homes,[3] even at the expense of watching a sea of other homes be consumed in their very own community.

This is the issue of lower-principled moral reasoning.

We have been conditioned to believe that there has to be an incentive at the end of our actions. We quite literally want to be paid in some form or another to be good to people.

This level of conditional love strips us of experiencing *tikkun olam*, a not-so-subtle reminder that we are morally obligated to engage in the sacred act of the slow (but necessary) betterment of society.

The most classic case of this idea was presented to me years ago in a unique way.

I was in the middle of nowhere Alabama, making my way into town with a friend. It was a long thirty minutes—no turns, no curves, no real sights to see. Just trailers, trees, and me and my buddy listening to Marcus King.

We were talking everything from church hurt to comedy to our favorite films and music. Then we took a hard, unexpected turn to theology. The words he spoke to me will stick to my heart and mind forever. He said:

> In the first and second centuries, there were creed keepers—people who were so fascinated with the life of Christ that they wrote down His every action and created laws for people in their communities to live by, based on His life and His character.[4]
>
> At the same time, there was another sect of people who carried themselves into the catacombs and painted His face in reverence . . . attempting to immortalize who Jesus was through the beauty in the pictures that they painted.[5]
>
> Who did it right?

All of this was news to me . . . so I sat there in silence for a moment, thinking, before I could muster a response. A few moments went by, and he spoke the answer for me.

> Both of them. The creed keepers weren't any more holy than the people who painted His face in the catacombs . . . they expressed

> His image in different ways, but the intentions of their heart were what mattered most.[6]

I genuinely had no clue how to respond. The words were so profound and timely.

They expressed *tikkun olam* by inadvertently working together to heal the wounds of the world.

A large part of *tikkun olam* is understanding how to adopt and express the different dimensions of a thing and its existence for the betterment of the world. It's refusing to see things only one way.

Regardless of their labels—creed keepers or creators in the catacombs—each of their efforts was necessary for the healing of the worlds within them and the world around them. Their existence (and their acts) were both expressions of eternity, and in committing to what they felt called to, we get a glimpse at the divinity that exists in their diversity.

They may have been fundamentally different in their acts of service, but the intentions, expressed with intimacy, left a legacy.

Admittedly, that conversation came at a very pivotal point in my faith journey.

I wanted to create and keep creeds in my life, to follow in the footsteps and teachings of Jesus. At the same time, I felt conflicted because other parts of me only wanted to create art and write about other parts of life that had nothing to do with my spiritual path or relationship with God. I was wrestling with whether my line of work was still worship . . . but this conversation gave me clarity.

God doesn't look down on me because of the life I live or the ways I choose to work or worship. In fact, it's all worship and should be seen as such. The silent or spoken judgment that comes from the eyes and ideas of others about how I choose to show up and help heal the world isn't even acknowledged or relevant in the eyes of God.

The truth is, we are all walking wounded, whether you can see the area of issue or not. *Tikkun olam* reminds us that repair rarely looks radical from the outside; instead, it often has ordinary beginnings.

You don't need an incentive to engage in loving ways with others. You don't need to share the same thoughts, feelings, and stances on every single issue you're faced with. You don't need a world that looks identical in order for it to be whole. Our task today is to embrace the efficacy within *tikkun olam*, slowly repairing the world through our perspective and the ways that we pursue peace in our everyday lives. Taking the first step into the uncomfortable, the unknown, and the unaccepted.

Today's poem—"I'm not cursed, I'm first"—means that being the first to embrace difference, to lead with love, and to see value in the diverse expressions of humanity is not a burden; it is a blessing.

It's an invitation to show others what is possible, to demonstrate that wholeness is found not in sameness but in the sacred dance of unity and diversity.

When we take that first step, we become partners in God's work of healing the wounds of the world, offering others the courage to do the same.

Shalom.

English, uh-mal-guh-MAY-shun

# 35 Amalgamation

The word *amalgamation* originates in the Middle Ages, pulled from the Medieval Latin *amalgama*, which referred to the process of blending mercury with another metal.[1] This metaphor of blending highlights the word's essence: to combine disparate elements into something unified, often resulting in a new, inseparable entity.

To experience or embody an *amalgamation* is to exist as someone or something that is made up completely of many complex layers and elements.

*More time spent assessing yourself will result in you accurately expressing yourself.*

If you've never seen the movie *Annihilation*,[2] put it on your watch list immediately.

It's one of my favorite films of all time, but more importantly, it's one of the most profound films I've encountered in my adulthood.

I am not someone who passively watches film or television. Call me quirky or eclectic, but I think critically and feel deeply. And I try to merge the two into something meaningful. For me, cinema is both a place of study and a playground for innovation.

When I watch movies or TV shows, I'm captivated not just by the obvious—like the plot or the visuals—but by the subtleties, the colors, the unspoken motifs, and the deliberate way the story unfolds. I take note of both the big, bold brushstrokes and the quiet whispers in the background.

*Annihilation* scratched every one of my cinematic itches. Based on a novel by Jeff VanderMeer, the film dives headfirst into the concept of amalgamation within the mysterious "Shimmer"—an otherworldly zone where biological life merges and mutates at a cellular level. Inside Area X, the boundaries between species and identities blur as flowers bloom in impossible shapes, human DNA fuses with flora and fauna, and the characters gradually lose themselves—literally and figuratively—to their environment.

At its heart, *Annihilation* is a meditation on identity, adaptation, and the tension between growth and destruction. When confronted with external forces beyond comprehension, the characters must reconcile their internal struggles with the chaos surrounding them. Some experience transformation, while others are entirely consumed.

The Shimmer becomes a haunting metaphor for life's pressures: a place where individuals either adapt, amalgamate, or disappear entirely.

In 2017, I stepped into my own kind of Shimmer. I had been invited to Atlanta for the first time to attend an event called "The Alternative." At the time, I was living in a peculiar in-between: Having just left a job in DC, I'd moved back to my college town to start graduate school, not because I had a clear vision for my future, but because I needed time. Atlanta, in contrast, felt alive and brimming with possibility.

The Alternative wasn't just an event . . . it was a movement.

What began as a gathering of three hundred young people in a train depot quickly swelled into a phenomenon, drawing thousands from across the country. It was electrifying, alive with lights, music, and passion. Yet, as I stood in the midst of it, I felt strangely disconnected. For someone from small-town West Virginia, the world of megachurch productions, celebrity pastors, and social-media ministry was surreal. It felt as if everyone around me was being reshaped by the environment—absorbing its culture, and mutating their dreams to align with the platform-driven vision of success it celebrated.

In *Annihilation*, the Shimmer doesn't ask permission to transform what enters it; it simply does.

DNA fuses, identities blur, and the boundaries between self and surroundings dissolve . . . and that's what I saw happening around me.

People I'd met months (and even years) before this platform began to pop off—people who once held personal, intimate dreams of obscurity—began aspiring to become influencers, preachers, podcasters, and church planters, not necessarily because it was their calling (or even what they felt momentarily called to), but because it was what the culture (that we helped create) exalted.

I slowly but surely watched the environment reshape them, mutating their ambitions into something they couldn't even fully recognize.

I heard recently that anything that skyrockets quickly has a deep potential to plummet just as fast... and that's exactly what I witnessed.

A year later, when the movement collapsed, so did many of those dreams.

But I wasn't swept up in the same wave; I kept surfing. Not because I was immune to the allure, but because I had spent time assessing what I truly wanted. I didn't want to chase someone else's dream or be molded by the expectations of my environment. I wanted to remain true to myself, even if it meant standing apart. Preaching was cool, but I loved spoken-word poetry. Watching my friends sign book deals was beautiful, but I prioritized writing words to instrumental music at cool cafés with company over the pressure to perform and manipulate my way into a manuscript. Seeing my colleagues crush it on social media, having viral moment after viral moment, was wonderful, but I could tell that the lives that they were living or aspiring toward weren't necessarily the desires that my heart wanted to home in on.

Like the characters in *Annihilation*, I understood the danger of amalgamation without intention—it can consume you, leaving behind a version of yourself that no longer belongs to you.

And that's the lesson I want to leave with you: Be careful when you dream.

The Shimmer of life is subtle and seductive, but it comes with the pressure to conform, to absorb the desires of others, and ultimately to pursue what's popular within whatever culture is calling cool in a moment.

But real dreams don't come from outside. They don't belong to the environment. They are born within you, in the quiet spaces where your heart speaks truth. That's why I say: "More time spent assessing yourself will always result in you accurately expressing yourself."

The otherworldly nature of amalgamation is that it can create something beautiful or something unrecognizable. The difference is discovered in our intentions.

So pause. Look inward. Ask yourself: Are these my dreams, or am I living out the script of someone else's story?

Remember, the life you build should reflect your authentic self—not a reflection of the culture, the crowd, or the Shimmer that surrounds you.

This is not an encouragement toward isolation or cynicism; it's a call to clarity.

Now is the perfect time to discern the origin of your intentions.

Is the dream rooted in your intimacy with God, or in your proximity to applause?

We are each uniquely wired, not just to protect our individuality, but to contribute something irreplaceable to the world around us.

When we discern rightly, we don't disappear from culture; we add depth to it. And in doing so, we make room to celebrate others, too, even if their rise looks different from ours.

There's nothing more sacred than a life fully, truly your own.

Shalom.

(שֶׁקֶר), Hebrew, sheh-KER

# 36 Sheqer

To lie, deceive, or feed one a falsehood. The Hebrew word *sheqer* is not simply about telling a lie; it is about living one.

It is the slow erosion of truth beneath the weight of convenience. It is the deception we offer others and the denial we offer ourselves. It is the moments when we abandon what is difficult for what is easy, when we rewrite history to avoid accountability, when we call disconnection "peace" because facing the fractures would require too much of us. *Sheqer* is not just falsehood—it is the comfort of falsehood, the lie that feels easier to live with than the truth.

And perhaps one of the most insidious forms of *sheqer* is the belief that we do not need each other. That the ache of our isolation is evidence of our independence rather than proof of our design.

*Despite what I believe*

*and despite what*

*I've been taught*

*my feelings are just feelings*

*and my thoughts are*

*just thoughts.*

Every day, we oscillate between peace and pain. And yet, when the balance tips toward pain, our first instinct is often to retreat—to cut ties, to close off, to convince ourselves that leaving is liberation.

Kurt Vonnegut wrote:

> Why are so many people getting divorced today?
>
> It's because most of us don't have extended families anymore. It used to be that when a man and a woman got married, the bride got a lot more people to talk to about everything. The groom got a lot more pals to tell dumb jokes to . . .
>
> But most of us, if we get married nowadays, are just one more person for the other person. The groom gets one more pal, but it's a woman. The woman gets one more person to talk to about everything, but it's a man.
>
> When a couple has an argument nowadays, they may think it's about money or power or sex or how to raise the kids or whatever. What they're really saying to each other, though without realizing it, is this: "You are not enough people!"[1]

I have sat with this quote for years.

In friendships. In work. In faith. In love.

I have felt the tension of needing more than what one person could provide, and I have watched as others, overwhelmed by that same reality, chose to leave rather than learn how to stay. This is not to say that every departure is unwarranted. Some separations are necessary; some endings are holy.

But I have come to believe that many of the fractures we experience are not because we are irreconcilable but because we are undisciplined. Because we have not been trained to sit in discomfort. Because we have mistaken discomfort for dysfunction.

We live in a culture that teaches us to prioritize our personal peace at all costs, but what if the cost is connection? What if the very thing we seek—to feel known, to feel understood, to feel safe—is only found on the other side of endurance?

My first book, *Humanity's Table*, was an attempt to answer this question. It was written out of necessity, in a time when I was watching the world slip further into isolation. The COVID-19 pandemic had not yet begun, but even then, I could feel the distance growing. *We had become a people who abandoned the table when the conversation got too complicated, who left the room instead of learning how to remain.*

My book was never about forcing people to agree—it was about encouraging them to stay. To believe that there was something sacred about sitting with one another, even when the meal was bitter. To understand that discomfort is not a sign to flee but a sign to lean in.

And yet, we are masters at avoidance. We have perfected the art of exit. In dating we call it *ghosting*. In marriage we call it *irreconcilable differences*. In politics we call it *polarization*.

We find new language for the same old instinct—to disappear when staying would demand too much of us.

But I do not want to be a person who disappears.

I do not want to be a person who bows to *sheqer*, who convinces myself that my comfort is more important than my calling to community. I do not want to trade endurance for ease, or patience for preference.

Because the truth is, I am not enough people either.

I need others to teach me what I do not know. To sharpen me. To challenge me. To remind me that my perspective is not the only one worth holding.

And so, I return to the table.

Not because it is easy. But because it is necessary.

Not because I always want to. But because I have learned that the alternative—the slow drift into disconnection—is not worth the illusion of peace it promises.

If *sheqer* is the lie that tells us we are better off alone, then *shalom* is the truth that tells us we never were.

So here is my invitation: If no one else has extended you one, here is your seat at the table.

A place to be. To wrestle. To wonder. To disagree and to stay anyway.

So maybe the challenge is this: Even if you're unable to return to the table—expand it.

Seek out someone who sees the world differently. Someone who votes differently, prays differently, parents differently, dreams differently—someone whose existence is just *different*.

Sit with them.

Listen without defense.

Disagree without distance.

Because connection isn't always about comfort. Sometimes, it's about courage.

And maybe what heals us is not perfect alignment but holy proximity—choosing to stay close even when we don't see eye to eye.

Shalom.

Cajun-French, LAN-yap

# 37 Lagniappe

A small, unexpected gift or bonus, often given out of generosity or goodwill.[1]

In the heart of Southern Louisiana, *lagniappe* is more than a word; it is a way of life. It is the extra beignet placed in the bag at a café, the handful of fresh herbs slipped into your basket at the market, the kindness that arrives unprompted, simply because it can.

But *lagniappe* is not just about receiving more—it is about the spirit in which it is given. It is an act that defies transactionality, a quiet rebellion against the economy of *just enough*. It does not ask, "What do I owe?" but rather, "What can I offer?" It is rooted in the belief that abundance is not measured in accumulation but in generosity. That love, when it is real, always spills over the edges.

This is the beauty of *lagniappe*—it transforms excess into offering. It invites us to see life not as something to be hoarded but as something to be handed out freely, with joy. And yet, it requires a posture that is rare in a world that trades in scarcity: *gratitude*.

*Gratitude alleviates the ailment of entitlement.*

There is something sacred about the hands that give freely. Not out of excess, but out of knowing. Not because they have much, but because they have experienced what it means to have little.

My friend Rich Perez once shared a truth that has never left me:

> It's typically those who give in excess that had to be given in excess. If you're the giver of generous grace, you probably had to be given grace generously. Same with love—you were deficient, and someone showed you what it meant to give it, so you replicate. Your cup is overflowing from your experiences, so you generously give because you know what it means to be given to.[2]

This is the heart of *lagniappe*—giving beyond what is required because you understand, firsthand, what it means to receive. And nowhere is this more evident than in the early church, where generosity was not an occasional virtue but a way of being.

We're about to take a hard turn here, so hang on.

In the Greco-Roman world, infanticide was common practice. If a child was born with a deformity, if they were unwanted, if their existence disrupted the family's financial stability or reputation, they were often discarded—left in fields, outside city gates, exposed to the elements. To the empire, a child's worth was conditional, contingent upon their utility. Their right to live was tied to their ability to fit within the societal mold.[3]

But the first Christians (specifically some of those in Ephesus), convicted by the Spirit of God and compelled by something deeper than law or tradition, did something radical. They went to those places—the margins, the outskirts, the forgotten spaces where life had been abandoned—and they gathered the children that society shunned and shut away.[4]

They did not need a government decree to tell them what was right. They did not need cultural permission to care. They didn't need some man with a megaphone to shout it at them. They simply knew that *love required action.*

This was their *noblesse oblige*, a French phrase that translates to "nobility obligates."[5] This is an emphasis on the idea that privilege and power come with the inherent responsibility to act with generosity, honor, and moral leadership. It suggests that those who have been given much, whether in wealth, status, or talent, are duty-bound to use their advantages for the good of others rather than for self-indulgence.

These acts were not born of aristocracy but of holy conviction. They understood that privilege, in whatever form it appeared, was not meant for hoarding but for healing.

That abundance was not about accumulation but about redistribution. And so, they took in the abandoned, raised the unwanted, and poured out what they had because they knew what it meant to lack.

This is where context for Christianity makes such a diligent difference.

I know it has been marred by the strong-arming of society through governmental abuse and proselytization. I know pastors and leaders in the church have muddied up the spaces and places of God because of the hindrances of their humanity. I know there's been unjust action that has interrupted the collective ability to commune with God.

But herein lies the opportunity to give an honest representation, a reorienting of the way that people see and experience the love and name of God and His goodness.

Even the smallest kindness, offered in secret, carries an echo that the world can feel.

Refusing to hold back is holy when it comes to extending compassion and kindness to others.

When we witness hoarding of any kind, there's typically a hidden ailment that needs to be addressed.

When a man or woman hoards their money and neglects the need to give cheerfully, there's a point of pain hidden somewhere in there. When a person polices another's personality and is upset by seeing someone else shine, there's an insecurity silently soaking inside them. When a Christian intentionally hides the love of God and advertently chooses who is worthy of it and who isn't, they've sadly released the necessary essence of eternity.

The antidote to all of these ailments? Gratitude.

Generosity is not just about resources—it is about presence.

It is about the willingness to pour out, to step toward the margins, to give from a place of knowing. Gratitude is the posture that dismantles the fear of lack, that interrupts the hoarding of love, that reminds us that *what we have was never meant for us alone*.

When the cup is full and spilling at the sides . . . the only question is: Why are you waiting to pour? When the cup is empty and punctured with holes . . . the question is: Who can you call on to ask for help that could lead you to the healing that you need?

Shalom.

Latin, TEM-ploom

# 38 Templum

A root of the English word *contemplation*.[1] It originally described a piece of consecrated ground, a sanctuary set apart for divine connection. In ancient Rome a *templum* was not merely a structure—it was a space designated for observing the heavens, a sacred vantage point where priests sought divine signs. Over time, the word came to signify more than a physical place; it became synonymous with an internal posture—a seat of secret revelation, where wisdom is received, not forced.[2]

To *contemplate* is to carve out a sacred space within ourselves. It is to pause, to listen, to wait for what cannot be rushed. In a world that demands movement, contemplation calls us to stillness. In a time that rewards reaction, contemplation insists on revelation. It is the unseen architecture of the soul's temple, where we meet God in the quiet, in the questions, in the spaces between words.

*God, please bring*

*us back to the*

*basics of being.*

All of life is integration: discovering parts of yourself as you experience life and its lessons, and finding ways to fit each new discovery into the dense, developed parts of your personality.

As we integrate, we also experience *dis*integration—the stripping away of ourselves. Especially those of us who are attempting to draw near to God. We know God's Spirit is a mirror of our humanity, and sometimes what we see needs to be stripped, because if we're not careful, we'll attempt to integrate things into our lives that come equipped with their own selfish, sinful interests.

We've all heard John 3:16: "For God so loved the world that he gave his one and only Son, that whoever believes in him shall not perish but have eternal life."

It's still as beautiful today as it was the first time I was ever introduced to it. But let's inspect it and see something new today. Perishing, in a theological context, has to do with being outside the presence of God. If God is light and our actions and intentions draw us closer to illumination, sin is the thing that casts us away from His presence and ultimately into the shadows.

Walking outside of the will of God leads to the promise of perishing.

In my personal life I can tell when I'm experiencing the shadows, because I certainly don't feel like myself. When I am stuck in unhealthy patterns of thought or practices that appease my flesh. When I'm stuck in a shame spiral and can't find my way out. When I'm thinking too introspectively and considering only myself, intentionally isolating myself from those I love.

I am disintegrating.

Di-*sin*-tegrating.

My lifestyle and choices, when not influenced by God's nature, beauty, and desires, lead me to feel and ultimately live as less of myself.

When this happens, I have to *re*integrate, and reintegrating requires intentionality and information—information that alleviates my burdens and encourages me back into the place of God's presence.

Theologian and author Richard Foster puts it this way:

> Within all of us is a whole conglomerate of selves . . . and all of these selves are rugged individualists . . . each one screams to protect his or her vested interests. If a decision is made to spend a relaxed evening listening to Chopin, the business self and the civic self rise up in protest at the loss of precious time. The energetic self paces back and forth, impatient and frustrated, and the religious self reminds us of the lost opportunities for study or evangelistic contact . . . no wonder we overcommit our schedules and live lives of frantic faithfulness.[3]

I hate to admit it, because it comes with such an ugly gut check, but this is us.

All of us.

Living lives of frantic faithfulness, committing ourselves to cause after cause, planning plan after plan—doing all that we can to appease ourselves and serve the many interests of self.

Containing multitudes requires us to sit with self and ask what we need now.

This has become so hard for us as a people because of the demands required of everyday life and the speed at which we choose to live. We need a reset. A standard that we succumb to, one that prioritizes efficiency and peace over speed and success. We need what Dr. Carl Jung referred to as the experience of "deep time," where we're so patient and present without distraction that it feels like time is standing still.[4] It is only in spaces like this, where we can contemplate and commune, that the answers we so desperately seek arise from the secret place within.

There was a time when stillness was woven into the rhythm of life. Before endless notifications, before the pressure to produce, before silence became something to be feared rather than welcomed.

Ancient wisdom tells us that contemplation was never passive; it was an act of radical openness, a deliberate retreat into sacred ground, whether external or internal. The Latin *templum* reminds us that space must be set apart before anything can be truly seen. The ancients would mark out a place, lift their eyes to the sky, and wait. Not to control but to understand. Not to impose meaning but to receive it.

Have we lost our *templum*?

I don't think we have, but I'm convinced that it's buried beneath the avalanche of everyday, and it's our duty to set out on a rescue mission to recover what we can of it and rebuild it back to its beauty.

If the ancient *templum* was a space for divine sight, then our own inner sanctuaries must be cultivated in the same way.

We do not sit in silence because we have time. We sit in silence because we need clarity. Because without stillness, the inner symphony of stress only grows louder. Without stillness, we remain fragmented, responding to competing selves instead of a unified soul.

But contemplation invites us back. To center. To clarity. To the basics of being.

This is not just a personal discipline—it is a cultural necessity.

We don't just need individuals who contemplate. We need communities who do.

Because without sacred spaces, we become scattered souls.

Without pause, we produce idols.

Without presence, we perform instead of perceive.

So many of our relationships suffer because we don't know how to sit with ourselves, let alone sit with others without needing to fix, prove, or escape.

But what if contemplation is the first act of connection? What if the way we return to ourselves is how we begin to return to one another?

This world does not need more noise. It needs more people willing to be quiet enough

to hear what heaven is saying—not just for their sake, but for ours.

The rebuilding of the *templum* starts with one soul, but it echoes into many.

So let us build the sanctuary again—not with hands, but with intention. Let us mark out the sacred space, step inside, and wait.

There is something to be heard. But only if we are quiet enough to listen.

Shalom.

(разблюто), Russian, RAZ-bli-oo-tow

# 39 Razbliuto

The quiet vacancy where love used to live. *Razbliuto* is not heartbreak—it is what comes after. When the ache has dulled, and the story no longer stings, but neither does it sing. It is the realization that something once full has emptied, and not with fury but with fading. There is no drama, no decisive end—just distance. Just silence.

It is a strange sort of grief, when even your sorrow starts to forget. *Razbliuto* speaks to the echo that remains after affection has vanished—not bitter, not sweet, only gone. And sometimes, that emptiness is the most honest thing we can name.

*We glorify the beauty of building and often demonize the duty of deconstruction.*

There's something beautiful about watching a foundation unfold. Laying the concrete of belief, applying the pillars of trust, setting up the scaffold to support what is being structured. Albeit unpretty when the building begins, we hold out hope for beauty as whatever is to come, becomes.

It's not just faith either. It's relationships, our personal life, and professional work. The goals that we set and the people we pursue. Ultimately, it's the program we accept as our life—some of it forced upon us, other parts freely adopted.

But what happens when you find fault in the system you exist within? When the setting is doing more damage than development? What happens when concerns and questions arise?

Do you put your head down and barrel on out of principle? Or do you put the car in Park, identify the issues, and find a way to manage the damage while continuing in discovery?

Deconstruction has become wildly popular among people of the Western Christian faith.

Deconstruction is often mischaracterized as rebellion (and in some cases it may be), but in reality, it can be the ultimate act of reverence—an unwillingness to accept shallow answers in place of deep, abiding truth.

For many, the journey of faith begins with an inherited framework, a system of beliefs handed down through culture, family, or tradition. This initial foundation, though necessary, is not immune to cracks. Some begin to notice inconsistencies, wrestle with painful experiences, or encounter perspectives that challenge what once felt certain. And for those who feel the tremors of doubt, it is not a mark of failure but of faith itself—the kind of faith that refuses to settle for an illusion of stability when true security can come only through testing and refining.

To dismiss or condemn this process is to misunderstand the very nature of faith. Scripture itself is filled with those who questioned, wrestled with, and reoriented their beliefs—not as an abandonment of God, but as a pursuit of Him.

Yet curiosity is often met with resistance. Some fear that questioning will lead to unraveling, believing that those who reevaluate their faith are discarding it altogether. But faith was never meant to be stagnant. It is a living, breathing reality, one that demands engagement, recalibration, and, at times, reconstruction.

A faith that is never examined may remain intact, but will it remain true? The heart set on knowing God must remain open to discovery, even when that discovery shifts expectations. To move forward in faith does not mean discarding the past, nor does it mean clinging to every part of it without discernment. It means sifting through, holding on to what is good, and allowing what is no longer life-giving to be released. And in this, there should be no shame—only the sacred invitation to walk more fully into the truth, even if it arrives in a form we did not anticipate.

My worldview was reoriented when I grasped what Jesus was saying in His Sermon on the Mount regarding the abundant life:

> You're blessed when you're at the end of your rope. With less of you there is more of God and his rule.
>
> You're blessed when you feel you've lost what is most dear to you. Only then can you be embraced by the One most dear to you.
>
> You're blessed when you're content with just who you are—no more, no less. That's the moment you find yourselves proud owners of everything that can't be bought.
>
> You're blessed when you've worked up a good appetite for God. He's food and drink in the best meal you'll ever eat.

> You're blessed when you care. At the moment of being "care-full," you find yourselves cared for.
>
> You're blessed when you get your inside world—your mind and heart—put right. Then you can see God in the outside world.
>
> You're blessed when you can show people how to cooperate instead of compete or fight. That's when you discover who you really are, and your place in God's family.
>
> You're blessed when your commitment to God provokes persecution. The persecution drives you even deeper into God's kingdom.
>
> Not only that—count yourselves blessed every time people put you down or throw you out or speak lies about you to discredit me. What it means is that the truth is too close for comfort and they are uncomfortable. You can be glad when that happens—give a cheer, even!—for though they don't like it, *I* do! And all heaven applauds. And know that you are in good company. My prophets and witnesses have always gotten into this kind of trouble. (Matthew 5:3–12 MSG)

I'm not sure what this sounds like to you, but to me, this is a very inverted idea of the abundant life. This couldn't be further from what I understood faith to be in my early life.

I believed I had to please God with my every action; there was no room for error. My mistakes were covered by grace, but it felt to me like it came on contingency.

My adulthood, my maturation in this faith that I've followed for so long, came with heartbreak that could only be fixed through restructuring my eyes and aligning them with the actuality of my lived experience. And it's the same with so many other people across the landscape of humanity too.

This is where *razbliuto* meets faith. It is one thing to lose love—it is another to realize it has simply faded. That what once stirred passion now feels distant, not through betrayal, but through time. Many walk through deconstruction only to arrive at this realization: The faith they once had is no longer what it used to be. And perhaps, that is okay.

Paul Ricœur speaks of the *second naivete*, a return to faith after deconstruction—not as blind belief, but as an earned trust.[1] If *razbliuto* is the cooling of love, then second naivete is the warming of wisdom. It is the realization that while certain things have faded, something deeper remains. Faith does not have to feel the way it did before to still be real. In fact, faith that has been tested and reassembled often holds more depth than one that was merely inherited.

The abundant life, then, is not in avoiding questions but in embracing them. It is not in resisting change but in walking through it with courage. It is not in the desperate attempt to return to an earlier version of belief but in allowing faith to evolve, to deepen, to take on a new shape—one that is honest, one that is rooted, and one that can stand through both the tearing down and the rebuilding.

So if you are questioning, let it be known: You are not failing—you are faithfully paying attention.

Make room for curiosity.

Let it become your spiritual discipline.

Because when we ask honest questions, we make space for honest answers.

And the Spirit of God is not afraid of either.

To those walking alongside others in this journey—be gentle.

Deconstruction is not disobedience.

Sometimes it is the purest form of devotion.

Let us be a people who welcome the wrestle.

Shalom.

(גַּם זוּ לְטוֹבָה), Hebrew, gahm zoo luh-TOH-vah

# 40 Gam zu l'tovah

*Gam zu l'tovah*, meaning "this, too, is for the good," is a phrase rooted in Jewish tradition, often used in times of difficulty or trial. It originates from a Talmudic sage, who was known for his unwavering faith. He was convinced that every event—whether joyful or painful—was ultimately for the greater good.[1]

Unlike simple optimism, this phrase carries a profound theological and philosophical depth. It does not dismiss suffering but instead acknowledges that even hardship has a purpose, often revealed only with time. It is a reminder of trust in divine orchestration, resilience in adversity, and the wisdom found in surrendering to the unknown.

*We want the benefit of healing without dealing with the hardship of our hurts.*

I am someone who is always looking for God. I mean always.

In the airport, at the coffee shop, in restaurants, and in conversations—I am innately convinced that God is everywhere, moving in everyone, able to do anything . . . and whatever fun He's having or story He is stirring up, I admittedly want to be a part of it in any way that I can.

I don't always do it well, or honestly know what I'm doing half the time, but my eyes and ears stay open often, as does my heart.

Although I love surprises and sweet moments of unforeseen story, I like to live in expectation—somewhere in between is where I see God move the most.

For example, a few years ago, I am making my way into a conference hall for registration, simply picking up my credentials and examining what and who will be where I am for the weekend.

There are many names I know, and many that I don't know—so I settle into the environment and attempt to get as acclimated as an introvert can.

Out of the corner of my eye, I see a Black man. He's about six feet tall, slender, and exceptionally reserved. I keep my space because I respect a man enjoying his solitude—I find a quiet corner and begin to do the same.

The conference was relatively small—there were maybe two hundred attendees—and we had intimate access to the speakers in the middle of their sessions and afterward, as the moderators encouraged dialogue. Many times my curiosity and zeal led me to the middle of the room, to the microphone, to ask questions and seek some sort of resolve from these voices I revered.

We arrive at the last day of the conference, and the last session is set to start. I'm in a bit of a rush, leaving the same registration hall that I walked in just days ago, when someone gently grabs me by my arm. I turn to see who it is, and it's the same guy I saw just several days prior—six feet tall, slender, off in the corner minding his business. I can see in his eyes that he's carrying a message . . . and what he shared would shape the next few years of my life. He said:

> Man, God adores you. You are like a Daniel. I can tell your curiosity and charisma exist to open the eyes and hearts of other people—to help them see eternity. I know you're eager to understand what God is doing in your life, and even more eager to understand how He's going to do it. But trusting Him in the unknown will help you embrace His promise when it's presented to you.
>
> It will be just like those pictures we used to get in grade school . . . the ones with the dots identified by numbers. You'd have to connect dot one to two, two to three, and you'd get glimpses of the image being created one dot at a time, not seeing what you've been drawing all along until you finally connect the last dot. That's how God is going to show it to you.

I was absolutely floored.

Tears began to well up in my eyes, and I reached out to him to shake his hand, and ultimately to give him a hug. I felt so seen in that moment. In a room filled with relevant names of faith, many folks striving to be seen and eager to be influential, I showed up, observed, asked questions, and got a gentle wink from God in this powerful, prophetic word.

It meant so much in the moment, but prophecy still has to crystallize over time and come to pass if it's true.

Fast-forward a few years later to 2024 . . . the most difficult year of my life. A year in which I would endure anxiety, financial hardship, a lack of professional progress, and what felt like a spiritual standstill.

I had put in so much work; I mean *so* much work. I'd written and published two books in the last several years. I'd written and directed a handful of documentary films. Started a successful podcast. Stood on hundreds of stages in both spiritual and secular spaces discussing a wide range of topics to diverse audiences.

The experiences were formative, and I felt like I was flourishing . . . but I couldn't see or feel the fruits of my labor.

In David Brooks's book *The Second Mountain*, he shares a theory about our early lives and how many of us accumulate material on the way up, having our lives shaped by status and success. On the way up this first mountain, you can and will accumulate material things . . . things that seem meaningful but are ultimately just tools in your belt to help you move up the most important mountain: the second one.

On the first mountain of life, while you're accumulating your material and seeking status and success, you miss out on service and the development of your soul. You aren't becoming service-oriented or exposed to life outside of your preferences or program. On the second mountain, however, you begin to see and experience the depths of reality, the beauties of God, and the unforeseen experiences that make life worth living.[2]

These mountains for me were inverted. I had the internal elements, but the external ones weren't present. I'd been spiritually formed through struggle and strife, but I didn't have external objects to symbolize that form of success. I'd had words of wisdom and lived a life filled with lessons that I'd shared with those around me, shaping my community and also my character, but there's no metric for meaning in those things.

I wanted something to show for how hard I'd worked, for how far I'd come. I wanted a reward for my efforts; I wanted a harvest of fruits for my labor. And over the course of that year, at the very end, I'd get everything I asked and prayed for. God would show me the full image He'd been piecing together all along, but not without the lessons learned through hurt and hardship that would shape the way I internalized and appreciated my inheritance.

And maybe you've been there too—doing everything right, holding nothing back, but still wondering when your moment will arrive. Maybe you're in the middle of connecting the dots, wondering if they'll ever form something worth seeing.

If so, you're not alone. And you're not off track.

But here is something significant to consider.

Sometimes we're scanning the branches for fruit, while heaven's attention is buried in the soil, working at the roots. The visible harvest matters far less than the unseen health beneath it. What we call delay might simply be God pulling up anything that could strangle the very blessing we've been praying for.

Meaning, while we're looking for external validation and the offering we believe we're owed, God is examining our internal world and attempting to uproot anything that will restrict the rewards and gifts He wants to give us.

How terrible would it be to degrade the upgrade.

To overlook or not appreciate our inheritance.

To squander our portion as a result of poor perspective.

To manufacture a blessing and strip God of His glory in our emotion and impatience.

It is a holy tension—to trust that love sometimes looks like endurance, that God's goodness is often disguised as discipline, and that the seasons of hardship we endure are not detours but divine designs. We long for ease, for swift rewards, for proof that our labor was not in vain.

But *gam zu l'tovah* does not promise immediate clarity; it invites us to hold fast when understanding is still forming, when the picture remains incomplete. It asks us to believe that God is just as present in the breaking as He is in the blessing.

Perhaps this is what it means to truly walk by faith—to trust that the unseen hand is still guiding, that every ache, every delay, and every unanswered prayer are leading us somewhere necessary.

If love is as much about formation as it is about fulfillment, then maybe divine love is not just in what we receive but in what we are stretched to become. And so, we say shalom—not just as a farewell, but as a declaration of wholeness, even in the waiting.

I used to think formation was a solo journey. But I've learned that endurance is communal.

It's not just God who meets us in the waiting—it's people too.

The friends who remind us of promises when we forget, the strangers who become messengers, the ones who see our growth even before we do.

Our healing rarely happens in isolation.

And neither does our becoming.

Shalom.

# Acknowledgments

To Rich Perez, Jose Reyes, Adam Thomason, Andy Mineo, and Terry Brown Jr. —

Thank you for being incredible men of God who gave me wisdom without condescension, grace without condition, and friendship without performance. You each created safe spaces for me to wrestle with questions, sharpen my thinking, and grow without fear of humiliation.

You lent me language when my own words fell short and walked with me through seasons of struggling, never letting shame define the journey. You invested deeply—in my soul, my ideas, my emotions, and who I am as a man—and for that, I carry your voices with me.

To Jason Dyba, Stevie Browning, Matt Reynolds, Davis Cook, and Luke Cooley —

Thank you for sharpening me with honesty and generosity. You gave me opportunities to create when discipline failed me, platforms to speak when fear silenced me, and perspective when I couldn't see beyond myself.

Our conversations, our trips, and even the hard moments became reminders that creativity is both a gift and a responsibility. You reminded me that what we want for others is often what we are longing for ourselves, and in that reflection, you helped me continue coming home to myself.

To Jay and Katherine Wolf—

Thank you for inviting me into your family with open hands and open hearts.

With you, I learned the freedom of existing without performance or prerequisite. Through Hope Heals, you gave me space to expand my theology, test ideas, and grow into a fuller, more refined version of myself. Your authenticity, warmth, and humility helped me develop a vocabulary of hope, softening my heart and shaping my thought life. My gratitude for your influence runs deeper than I can say.

To Nick Roth and Kelly Willard—

Thank you for seeing me. Kelly, your kindness opened the door to the dream work I now get to do, in ways that only divine serendipity could orchestrate. Nick, your encouragement and affirmation gave me confidence when I struggled to believe in myself. Together, you've held space for me, believed in me, and given me the gift of being known. Because of your intentionality, I was able to step into a season I might never have reached without you.

To Carly Burruss, Hadassah Lynch, Gloria Umanah, and Kendra Stowe—

Thank you for being steady companions who brought both laughter and belief into my life.

With you, even the hardest seasons found lightness—we discovered the joke in nearly everything, yet never lost sight of faith in what was possible. You sat with me in disappointment and disbelief, holding space until what I longed for finally came to pass. Your encouragement, support, and humor were more than comfort; they were reminders that joy and hope often walk hand in hand.

# Notes

## Introduction

1. "How Many Languages Are There in the World?," Ethnologue, accessed June 29, 2025, https://www.ethnologue.com/insights/how-many-languages/.
2. Dominika Baran, "America's Bilingual Roots," *Language Magazine*, August 7, 2018, https://languagemagazine.com/2018/08/07/americas-bilingual-roots/.
3. Sean McGibney, "What Percentage of the World's Population Is Bilingual?," *Newsdle*, July 2023, accessed July 31, 2025, https://www.newsdle.com/blog/world-population-bilingual-percentage.
4. American Academy of Arts and Sciences, *The State of Languages in the U.S.: A Statistical Portrait*, December 2016, https://www.amacad.org/sites/default/files/academy/multimedia/pdfs/publications/researchpapersmonographs/State-of-Languages-in-US.pdf, 5.
5. Annisa RT, "Busting the Great 'Goldfish Attention Span' Myth," Medium, June 2, 2021, https://medium.com/better-marketing/busting-the-great-goldfish-attention-span-myth-8150ba9af0ef.
6. "Literacy Statistics 2024–2025 (Where We Are Now)," National Literacy Institute, accessed June 29, 2025, https://www.thenationalliteracyinstitute.com/2024–2025-literacy-statistics.
7. "Literacy Statistics 2024–2025 (Where We Are Now)."
8. "Peace-Shalom (Hebrew Word Study)," Precept Austin, last updated January 17, 2025, https://www.preceptaustin.org/shalom_-_definition.

## Entry 2

1. Emilia Lathi, "Embodied Fortitude: An Introduction to the Finnish Construct of Sisu," *International Journal of Wellbeing* 9, no. 1 (2019): 61–82, https://doi.org/10.5502/ijw.v9i1.672.
2. William Ernest Henley, "Invictus," Poetry Foundation, originally published 1875, accessed October 27, 2025, https://www.poetry foundation.org/poems/51642/invictus.

## Entry 3

1. *Merriam-Webster*, "vulnerable," accessed August 21, 2025, https://www.merriam-webster.com/dictionary/vulnerable.
2. Ancient Languages, "Vulnus, Vulneris," accessed July 31, 2025, https://ancientlanguages.org/latin/dictionary/vulnus-vulneris.

## Entry 5

1. Oliver Burkeman, *Four Thousand Weeks: Time and How to Use It* (Random House, 2021), 91.

## Entry 6

1. "The Dangerous Construction of Manhattan's Skyscrapers," Online Safety Trainer, February 19, 2023, https://www.onlinesafetytrainer .com/the-dangerous-construction-of-manhattans-skyscrapers/.
2. C. S. Lewis, *Mere Christianity* (Touchstone, 1996), 175–76.
3. Maya Angelou, "Caged Bird," Poetry Foundation, accessed July 30, 2025, https://www.poetryfoundation.org/poems/48989/caged-bird.

## Entry 7

1. Barbara Brown Taylor, *Learning to Walk in the Dark* (HarperOne, 2014), 47.

## Entry 8

1. "What Is Kaizen?—Meaning & Principles Explained," Lakshya Indian Institute of Commerce, updated June 21, 2025, https://lakshyacommerce.com/academics/kaizen.

## Entry 9

1. See, for example, Deuteronomy 20:8: "The officers shall speak further to the people, and say, 'What man is there who is fearful and fainthearted? Let him go and return to his house, lest the heart of his brethren faint like his heart'" (NKJV). Here, *rakak* is translated as "to be fainthearted," describing a heart that is tender or soft, susceptible to fear; 2 Kings 22:19: "Because your heart was tender, and you humbled yourself before the LORD when you heard what I spoke" (NKJV). In this verse, *rakak* is rendered as "was tender," referring to King Josiah's soft heart that was receptive to God's word, leading to humility and repentance; and 2 Chronicles 13:7: "Then worthless rogues gathered to him, and strengthened themselves against Rehoboam the son of Solomon, when Rehoboam was young and inexperienced and could not withstand them" (NKJV). The term "was inexperienced" translates *rakak*, indicating a softness or lack of firmness in leadership.
2. "Strong's Hebrew: 7390. רַךְ (Rak)—Tender, Soft, Delicate, Weak," BibleHub, accessed August 12, 2025, https://biblehub.com/hebrew/7390.htm; "Strong's Greek: 5543. χρηστός (chrēstos)—Good, Kind," BibleHub, accessed August 12, 2025, https://biblehub.com/greek/5543.htm.
3. Brother Lawrence, *The Practice of the Presence of God*, trans. Salvatore Sciurba (ICS Publications, 1994), 115.

## Entry 10

1. *Merriam-Webster*, "genuflect," accessed July 30, 2025, https://www.merriam-webster.com/dictionary/genuflect.
2. Rund Abdelfatah, host, *Throughline*, podcast, "James Baldwin's Fire," NPR, September 17, 2020, https://www.npr.org/transcripts/912769283.

## Entry 11

1. Charles Duhigg, "The Habit Loop," chap. 1 in *The Power of Habit: Why We Do What We Do in Life and Business* (Random House, 2012).
2. Daniel Pauly, "The Ocean's Shifting Baseline," TED Talk, YouTube video, April 2010, 8 min., 45 sec., https://www.ted.com/talks/daniel_pauly_the_ocean_s_shifting_baseline; Heidi K. Alleway

et al., "The Shifting Baseline Syndrome as a Connective Concept for More Informed and Just Responses to Global Environmental Change," *People and Nature* 5, no. 3 (June 2023): 885–96, https://doi.org/10.1002/pan3.10473.

## Entry 13

1. *Dark Matter*, season 1, episode 7, "In the Fires of Dead Stars," directed by Roxann Dawson, aired on June 12, 2024, on Apple TV+.

## Entry 14

1. The Minimalists, *The Minimalists Private Podcast*, podcast, episode 388, "Money Clutter," April 17, 2023, https://www.theminimalists.com/podcast/.

## Entry 15

1. "Perceptual Positions: Powerful Exercise to Strengthen Understanding and Empathy," Trainers Toolbox, accessed June 30, 2025, https://www.trainers-toolbox.com/perceptual-positions-powerful-exercise-to-strengthen-understanding-and-empathy/.

## Entry 16

1. Stephen Langdon, trans., The Epic of Gilgamish (University Museum, 1917), accessed July 31, 2025, via Project Gutenberg, https://www.gutenberg.org/ebooks/18897.
2. "Humbristic to Humble Gilgamesh Analysis," IPL, accessed June 30, 2025, https://www.ipl.org/essay/Humbristic-To-Humble-Gilgamesh-Analysis-PC7W9HUYV.

## Entry 17

1. *Encyclopedia Britannica*, "agape," accessed July 31, 2025, https://www.britannica.com/topic/agape.
2. Muhammad Muhammadi Rayshahri, *Al-Mahabbah fi al-Kitab wa al-Sunnah ("Love in the Book and Sunnah")*, 3rd ed., Arabic, Dar al-Hadith, Qom, Iran, 2003, as summarized on Hadith.net, accessed July 31, 2025, https://hadith.net/en/post/27949/al-mahabbah-fi-al-kitab-wa-al-sunnah/.

## Entry 18

1. Michael Amoruso, "Saudade: The Untranslatable Word for the Presence of Absence," *Big Think*, October 16, 2018, https://bigthink.com/the-present/saudade-the-untranslatable-word-for-the-presence-of-absence-2612653551/.
2. A. M. Hestbech, "Reclaiming the Inner Child in Cognitive-Behavioral Therapy: The Complementary Model of the Personality," *American Journal of Psychotherapy* 71, no. 1 (June 2018): 21–27, https://doi.org/10.1176/appi.psychotherapy.20180008.

## Entry 19

1. "Strong's Greek 3341: μετάνοια (Metanoia)," BibleHub, accessed July 31, 2025, https://biblehub.com/greek/3341.htm.

## Entry 20

1. Bad Bunny, *DeBÍ TiRAR MáS FOToS*, Rimas Entertainment, 2025.

## Entry 21

1. Online Etymology Dictionary, "humility," accessed July 1, 2025, https://www.etymonline.com/word/humility; *Merriam-Webster*, "humble," accessed July 1, 2025, https://www.merriam-webster.com/dictionary/humble.
2. *Merriam-Webster*, "behold," accessed July 1, 2025, https://www.merriam-webster.com/dictionary/behold.

## Entry 22

1. Kurt Vonnegut, *A Man Without a Country* (Seven Stories Press, 2005).
2. Vonnegut, *A Man Without a Country*, 68.

## Entry 24

1. John Koenig, *The Dictionary of Obscure Sorrows* (Simon & Schuster, 2021).
2. Charles H. Spurgeon, "Consolation Proportionate to Spiritual Sufferings," sermon, delivered March 11, 1855, Spurgeon's Sermons Vol. 01: 1855, Christian Classics Ethereal Library, accessed August 22, 2025, https://www.ccel.org/ccel/spurgeon/sermons01.xii.html.

## Entry 26

1. Farmer Sean, "Two Monks and a Woman—Zen Story," Medium, June 30, 2018, https://medium.com/@soninilucas/two-monks-and-a-woman-zen-story-c15294c394c1.

## Entry 27

1. BNESIM, "Resfeber, Fernweh, and Other Travel Words You've Never Heard Before," Medium, November 5, 2019, https://medium.com/@bnesim/resfeber-fernweh-and-other-travel-words-youve-never-heard-before-8d382cca0dc7.

## Entry 28

1. Pradeep Kumar Dhoopati, "The Mirror Principle," LinkedIn, August 5, 2023, https://www.linkedin.com/pulse/mirror-principle-pradeep-kumar-dhoopati/.

## Entry 30

1. Wendy Diaz, "Silence as a Means of Spiritual Enlightenment," The Message International, February 28, 2024, https://messageinternational.org/silence-as-a-means-of-spiritual-enlightenment/.
2. Dave Gibbons, phone conversation with author, Nashville, TN, September 21, 2021.
3. Rachel Faulkner Brown and Karen McAdams, hosts, *There Is More*, podcast, "Kingdom Solutions—Dubb Alexander Pt. 1," Spotify, March 25, 2024, https://creators.spotify.com/pod/profile/be-still-ministries/episodes/Kingdom-Solutions–Dubb-Alexander-Pt—1-e2hin8p.

## Entry 31

1. Jane Howard, "Telling Talk from a Negro Writer," *LIFE*, May 24, 1963, as quoted in Maria Popova, "The Doom and Glory of Knowing Who You Are: James Baldwin on the Empathic Rewards of Reading and What It Means to Be an Artist," *The Marginalian*, May 24, 2017, https://www.themarginalian.org/2017/05/24/james-baldwin-life-magazine-1963/.

## Entry 32

1. Martin Luther King Jr., "A Knock at Midnight," sermon, as quoted in "Martin Luther King, Jr. and the Power of Religious Conviction," First Liberty, January 16, 2023, https://firstliberty.org/news/martin-luther-king-jr-and-the-power-of-religious-conviction/.

## Entry 33

1. Edge Foundation, Inc., "2012: What Is Your Favorite Deep, Elegant, or Beautiful Explanation?," Edge.org, accessed July 31, 2025, https://www.edge.org/annual-question/what-is-your-favorite-deep-elegant-or-beautiful-explanation.

## Entry 34

1. Cynthia Tina, "Timeline of Intentional Communities," Foundation for Intentional Community, October 8, 2021, https://www.ic.org/timeline-of-intentional-communities/?srsltid=AfmBOopxCJ5922P6L3TcF9sVTi0OrSQNBYKu9Cuywpta5DqDfoLk4Zpi.
2. "The History of the Coliving Movement," Coliving.com, March 9, 2020, https://coliving.com/blog/what-is-behind-the-coliving-movement.
3. Laurel Wamsley, "Insurance Companies and Wealthy LA Residents Hire Private Firefighters for Protection," interview by Leila Fadel, *Morning Edition*, NPR, January 17, 2025, https://www.npr.org/2025/01/17/nx-s1–5258240/insurance-companies-and-wealthy-la-residents-hire-private-firefighters-for-protection.
4. Daniel Anderson, "Easter's Earliest Creed," Creation Ministries International, March 8, 2007, https://creation.com/en-us/articles/easters-earliest-creed.
5. Somapika Dutta, "7 Oldest Paintings of Jesus in the World," Oldest.org, March 17, 2025, https://www.oldest.org/artliterature/jesus-paintings/.
6. Dustin Nickerson, conversation with the author, Nauvoo, Alabama, at Hope Heals Camp, 2022.

## Entry 35

1. *Merriam-Webster*, "amalgamate," accessed July 2, 2025, https://www.merriam-webster.com/dictionary/amalgamate.
2. *Annihilation*, directed by Alex Garland (Paramount Pictures, 2018).

## Entry 36

1. Vonnegut, "You Are Not Enough People," chap. 5 in *A Man Without a Country* (Seven Stories Press, 2005).

## Entry 37

1. *Merriam-Webster*, "lagniappe," accessed July 2, 2025, https://www.merriam-webster.com/dictionary/lagniappe.
2. Rich Perez, conversation with the author, Atlanta, GA, 2022.
3. Louis Gosbell, "'As Long as It's Healthy': What Can We Learn from Early Christianity's Resistance to Infanticide and Exposure?," *ABC Religion & Ethics*, March 13, 2019, https://www.abc.net.au/religion/early-christianitys-resistance-to-infanticide-and-exposure/10898016.
4. Gregory Soderberg, "The Christian Compassion Revolution," BibleMesh, June 1, 2022, https://biblemesh.com/blog/the-christian-compassion-revolution/.
5. *Merriam-Webster*, "noblesse oblige," accessed July 2, 2025, https://www.merriam-webster.com/dictionary/noblesse%20oblige.

## Entry 38

1. Online Etymology Dictionary, "contemplation," accessed July 2, 2025, https://www.etymonline.com/word/contemplation.
2. Michael Glerup, "Contemplation: The Aim of the Christian Life," *Conversatio Divina*, fall 2006, accessed August 12, 2025, https://conversatio.org/contemplation-the-aim-of-the-christian-life; "Templum," *Ancient World 3D*, Indianapolis University Library Exhibits, accessed August 12, 2025, https://exhibits.library.indianapolis.iu.edu/aw3d/templum.
3. Richard Foster, *Freedom of Simplicity: Finding Harmony in a Complex World*, rev. ed. (HarperOne, 2005), 95–96.
4. Angeliki Yiassemides, "Synchronicity: Carl Jung's Principle for Understanding Time and Timelessness," January 13, 2023, https://www.angelikiyiassemides.com/en/news/synchronicity-principle-time-timelessness.

## Entry 39

1. Mark I. Wallace, *The Second Naiveté: Barth, Ricoeur, and the New Yale Theology* (Mercer, 1995); Grant Skeldon, "Deconstruction and Progressive

Christianity with John Mark Comer," YouTube, January 28, 2025, 33 min., 49 sec., https://www.youtube.com/watch?v=snX5kUaST5I.

## Entry 40

1. Nissan Mindel, "Nachum Ish Gamzu," Chabad.org, accessed August 4, 2025, https://www.chabad.org/library/article_cdo/aid/112506/jewish/Nahum-Ish-Gamzu.htm.
2. David Brooks, *The Second Mountain: The Question for a Moral Life* (Random House, 2019).

# About the Author

**Nigel Darius** is a storyteller, author, educator, and artist whose work is dedicated to revealing the beauty within humanity. Through his lectures, writing, art, and heartfelt conversations, Nigel invites us to see the world—and each other—more clearly, with deeper empathy and renewed curiosity.

Nigel's perspective aims to translate the complexities of the human experience into approachable narratives, often building bridges between the sacred and the secular, the personal and the universal. His work offers clarity, meaning, and hope amid the chaos of modern life.

When he's not creating, Nigel finds restoration through travel—exploring cultures, communities, and the beauty of creation. Local to Atlanta, he splits his time between Denver and Brooklyn, drawing inspiration from the vibrancy of the city, the people who populate it, and the necessity of nature on the outskirts.

Coffee, interior design, great wine, and meaningful conversations keep his cup full.

At his core, Nigel is driven by a profound belief—that wholeness and healing are available to all humanity.

His life is a testament to the power of living intentionally, connecting deeply, and discovering the divine in the everyday. For those seeking to learn, heal, and rediscover hope, Nigel Darius is a voice and presence you can trust to guide the way.